# AKASHIC RECORDS
## for Beginners

ANTHONY WILKINS

AKASHIC RECORDS

Copyright © 2019 Antony Wilkins

All rights reserved.

AKASHIC RECORDS

© *Copyright 2019 by Antony Wilkins*
*All rights reserved.*

*This document is geared towards providing exact and reliable information with regards to the topic and issue covered. The publication is sold with the idea that the publisher is not required to render accounting, officially permitted, or otherwise, qualified services. If advice is necessary, legal or professional, a practiced individual in the profession should be ordered.*
*- From a Declaration of Principles which was accepted and approved equally by a Committee of the American Bar Association and a Committee of Publishers and Associations.*
*In no way is it legal to reproduce, duplicate, or transmit any part of this document in either electronic means or in printed format. Recording of this publication is strictly prohibited and any storage of this document is not allowed unless with written permission from the publisher. All rights reserved.*
*The information provided herein is stated to be truthful and consistent, in that any liability, in terms of inattention or otherwise, by any usage or abuse of any policies, processes, or directions contained within is the solitary and utter responsibility of the recipient reader. Under no circumstances will any legal responsibility or blame be held against the publisher for any reparation, damages, or monetary loss due to the information herein, either directly or indirectly.*
*Respective authors own all copyrights not held by the publisher.*

# AKASHIC RECORDS

*The information herein is offered for informational purposes solely, and is universal as so. The presentation of the information is without contract or any type of guarantee assurance.*

*The trademarks that are used are without any consent, and the publication of the trademark is without permission or backing by the trademark owner. All trademarks and brands within this book are for clarifying purposes only and are the owned by the owners themselves, not affiliated with this document.*

# AKASHIC RECORDS

# CONTENTS

|   | | |
|---|---|---|
|   | INTRODUCTION | 1 |
| 1 | ACCESSING YOUR AKASHIC RECORDS | 4 |
| 2 | YOUR AKASHIC RECORD READER | 14 |
| 3 | WORKING WITH YOUR AKASHIC RECORD KEEPER | 18 |
| 4 | AKASHIC READING ON INCLUSION | 22 |
| 5 | THE HUMAN NATURE AND BEHAVIORS | 32 |
| 6 | ATTAINING CLARITY IN OUR PERCEPTIONS AND OUR SPIRITUAL JOURNEY | 45 |
| 7 | AKASHIC RECORDS ABOUT HUMAN SUCCESS AND THEIR FEAR | 58 |
| 8 | CONNECTING TO CONSCIOUSNESS AND SPIRITUALITY, CONTROL DIVERSITY WITH YOURSELF AND OTHER HUMANS | 69 |
| 9 | RECORDS OF CONNECTION AND CHANGES | 82 |
| 10 | RECORD CONNECTED TO LOVE AND PEACE OF MIND | 100 |
|   | CONCLUSION | 114 |

# INTRODUCTION

Through the concept of theosophy and anthroposophy, Akashic records are known to be the collections of all human activities, their ideas, imaginations, emotions, thoughts, and decisions that have happened in the past, the ones happening at the moment, and the future events. This concept is believed to be a coded idea by theosophists in a supernatural atmosphere known as etheric plane. It is also believed that there are anecdotal records, however, there's no tangible proof to show the existence of the Akashic records for the concept to be fully understood.

The Akashic Records is a concept that has been around for many years. The idea of a higher dimensional library was popularized by the 19th Century Theosophy movement. The Akashic Records are like a big library in the sky where your spirit stores its information in. Isn't this amazing?! The information about mankind and all their activities; in the past, present, and in future.

Recently, it has been revealed that the Akashic Records can be manipulated by certain classes of beings. The information held in those records is not infallible or absolutely secure. It is hard to say if that's going to affect the majority of people. Some people's claim to the level of manipulation of these libraries is much greater than others.

All our actions, thoughts and intentions are energetically recorded in a virtual database called the Akashic Records. Every Soul, from the time it has been created, has its own Akashic Record. Properties, pets, events and thoughts have their own records as well. During our reading session, I will help you to learn about your Soul identity and understand how it determines your life experiences. We will remove your Soul-level energetic blocks and restrictions that hold you back and prevent you from living your life at its best. This clearing process will result in profound positive changes on many levels - physical, mental, emotional and spiritual.

All our problems and negative life situations are not random events. They have common root causes - spiritual blocks and restraints that we have on the Soul level. When our Souls were created by the Divine, they were created in accordance with a "blueprint" which since has been corrupted by negative energies. As a result, when we physically incarnate our connection to the Divine source, it is not as strong as it may be. Consequently, we became vulnerable to dark influences. This in turn creates unwanted negative life experiences as well as numerous blocks and restrictions. These restrictions prevent us from living our lives, following our purpose for our highest good and highest good of all.

As your Akashic Records are held in the vibration of love for you, you can access them in those intuitive moments that you have. Every human has accessed their own records for themselves at different times in their lives. These moments are what humans call 'intuition' - you know, those moments when you just 'know' that you know something and you know that thing clearly. You may only be in this knowing of yourself for a moment. It is in those moments that you are actually accessing your very own Akashic Records.

Most of the information people are interested in – past lives, soul purpose, life lessons, karma, relationship potentials, and many others can all be seen by clairvoyants by directly reading a person, perhaps through the minds or way of life. In other words, in many cases, there is no need to get a special Akashic Record reading. Most institutionally trained clairvoyants do not even offer these kinds of readings. Why read books in a library when you can go directly to the source? It's a question to be answered immediately without much gesture.

However, in the book, you will learn everything you need to know about your Akashic records and how to make the best out of it. The Akashic records discussed in this book will open your eyes and widen your understanding about your spirit being, how you can access some of your mystical realms and make good decisions about your life. Every man has his own Akashic records. It could be seen as a supernatural concept to use possible past occurrence to connote the present decisions for a better future.

The more intuitive you allow yourself to be, the more you can access your Akashic Records. For those of you who would like to have more of this knowledge, more of this information about yourself, you have the opportunity to gather this information through people who use their intuitive processes to access your Akashic Records. Pamela can do this, to access your Akashic Records and help you find out more about you really are, bringing through information from your Akashic Record Keepers as you have a conversation with them about yourself and your life.

As a matter of fact, Akashic records will systematically arrange your thoughts to make a good judgement about everything you're going through and things you will still go through in life. It's all about making you a better person. It's time to get started!

# 1 ACCESSING YOUR AKASHIC RECORDS

We should know that the Akashic Records are the thoughts of humans either in the past, present, or in the future. Through your Akashic Records, you can learn about the past by penetrating into it in your mind. This enables you to understand yourself better, even to the spirit realm. Even though this action often takes time, practice, and strategies to discover, yet you will definitely access the deepest part of the other side through simple meditation method. I will share with you fabulous accessing methods in which you can use to access your Akashic Records.

Here are the simple steps to access your Akashic Records:

1. **Focus on your search**

{A}. While focusing on your search, you need to know and understand your intentions and reasons why you're accessing your Akashic records. It's very expedient to think about it and understand the reason you're doing it. You should consider the exact thing you want to know, why you want to know it, and how the knowledge of the search will help you. Make sure you know this before you start anything. If you fail to understand what you want, you may end up being destabilized and confused. The moment you're destabilized, you will lose focus and end up missing the needed information available.

You may want to know possibly why you're hot tempered in order to learn how to control it. Also, in the aspect of career, you may want to know your goals so that you can make a good decision. At the same time, you may want to understand your core value, relationships with others, and the likes, so that you learn how to relate with others and connect with people you can flow easily with.

**POINT TO NOTE:** Always be patient with yourself to know the exact thing you're searching for in your Akashic Records. The level of your concentration will definitely determine the kind of result you will get. The better you focus on the things you want, the better result you have. You can write things down if need be. At the same time, you can talk to friends or read books to assist you in knowing the main reasons you want to access your Akashic records.

{B}.Think about your past and put something down.

You can make a full list of possible questions that

will assist you to get adequate information for what you're looking for. Do not confuse yourself too much with unnecessary bulky questions which may impact your search negatively. Focus on possible questions and topics that will help you to get the best information you need. For instance, you may want to consider questions like this, "Where did I meet my husband?" or "What type of jobs did I do in the past?" or "What type of tragedy have I experienced in the past?". These types of questions have great influence on our present life. You should think about questions or topics that can possibly connect our past to the present and eventually influence the future.

{C}.Make sure you don't deviate from possible questions that help you to make good decisions in your present life. Describe to yourself the kind of problem you've been struggling with, then seek the right information relating to it which will help you get a better clue. This strategy will assist you to easily navigate through your search in order to get adequate information that will further your understanding in knowing the relationship between your past and the present.

You can consider something like, "I want to move to a new environment, but each time this decision comes, I easily change my mind. Does it have anything to do with my past, and how can this help me to make a sincere decision?"

Perhaps, you may want to say, "Lately I've been struggling to trust my significant other. I feel that this is based on something more than I am aware of in my present life. If I am right, please hint me with the information on the exact time this happened and how it happened."

{D}. Try to ask one question at a time to focus

more on the exact thing you need in your search. This approach may enable you to gain clarity on an issue, similar to how you may want to focus on one aspect of your life at a time during a tarot card or palm reading. Focus on your relationships, career, health, and other personal interests one at a time.

For instance, you may want to start by asking in this format, "Is my relationship going to result in marriage or are we just too different for things to work out?"

Then, you might ask, "Will it be possible to get the needed promotion I have been working so hard to get, or will I have to wait for some other time?

2. **Enter into a Receptive State**

{A}. Start by stating and analyzing your intention or possible question aloud and ask for guidance. When you're set to start the approach of accessing your Akashic records, say what you're looking for out loud. Focus on the question or search query that you have developed. Segregate your attention and set it at the forefront of your mind so that you will be able to remain stable and focused on it during your search in your Akashic records.

Do not forget to put in mind to always state your question as accurately, specifically and specially as possible, such as, "What kind of professions have I had in my past lives that may help me to find what I should be in this life?"

{B}.Position yourself. Sit in a cool, comfortable, and quiet place. As a matter of fact, you might want to attempt to access your Akashic records anywhere or in a comfortable place you want, but it usually helps if you are not distracted or in a place that nothing will interrupt your search. You can consider doing this in your bedroom or your office when no one will interrupt, and with your door being closed. Also consider trying to do this early in the day, it could at night, or a period during the day in which nobody can be in a form of distraction. You also consider using pillows and either your blankets or clothes to make yourself comfortable and convenient.

**POINT TO NOTE:** If you're a little bit nervous, you can try starting with a little prayer like, "Dear God (if you believe in the creator), please guide me through as I start my search and encompass me around with your protective shield of perfect insight of illuminated light."

{C}. Focus your attention and maintain a stable state. You can begin by trying to close your eyes, this helps you to take about few minutes to breathe deeply. Breathe in through your nose to the count of about three to five, then hold for about some more seconds, and breathe out through your mouth by counting to a number of four to five as well. Maintain your steady breathing mechanism and pause for about five minutes or any time as long as it takes to get yourself into a state of deep relaxation for adequate concentration of your search. Don't forget to place your two hands on your stomach so that you can concentrate more on your breathing.

{D}. Meditate through on your topics or questions while you're relaxing. The moment you access that state of deep relaxation, clear your mind of all thoughts except for your question. Make sure you repeat all your questions and be focused. Most of the time, you will be distracted, don't worry, it's normal. If you notice your thoughts are a little bit straying or distracted by mere activities around, redirect yourself to your mantra and continue the process in order to maintain a stable meditation. Breathe deeply throughout the meditation.

{E}. Make an enquiry in order to be granted access to your Akashic records. The moment you have started meditating for about five minutes or longer, you can easily access the Akashic records. Get access and speak loud or maybe silently, "I want to know more about my past lives. Am I permitted to access the Akashic records to find what I want?" When you ask your question, maintain your breathing deeply in order to clear your mind.

You will probably hear things, feel, or see a response through the eyes of your mind. Do not worry, when you're not getting the answers you want. It can actually mean that you need to continue meditating and keep asking.

**POINT TO NOTE:** Don't forget that some people, accessing the Akashic records can try many ways. If you don't see any tangible result this time, don't be discouraged! Do not give up, keep trying and you will get the needed information you want.

{F}. Be patient and wait for information to come into your conscious mind. After you've positioned your question and request for access to the Akashic records out into the universe, all that's needed is to wait for an answer for the right to come. Maintain your breathing, concentrate on your meditation and remain receptive to any information that floats into your conscious mind as this may be coming from your Akashic record.

Bear in mind that the information can take on different forms. Your sensory neurons will be active, pay attention to them and you will get the needed.

For example, if you've asked about your profession in a previous life, you might see a hammer in your mind's eye, which could indicate that you were a carpenter or blacksmith. At the same time, you may feel some sweet taste, this will point that you're actually a baker.

**HERE'S A WARNING:** Be aware that you may receive information about what you were in a past life that could be disturbing. However, it's important to remain open to the information and avoid judging yourself for any past action to get the most out of your Akashic reading.

{G}. Introduce yourself and state your question to anyone you encounter after your search. Most often, when you're accessing the Akashic records, you may like to feel the presence of another being or soul nearby to you. The moment you feel this sign, introduce yourself and repeat your question again. The nearby being might be your guardian or keeper of the records who will possibly assist you to find the information you're looking for, or perhaps another soul whom you have known in a past life. Any of these clues may help you gain valuable information by taking a moment to introduce yourself and ask for assistance.

You can try and say something like this, "Hi, I am Tom and I am seeking information about any phobias I had been into in my past lives." I want you to help me fix and provide an answer to it.

3. **Translate things you got into what you understand**

{A}. Allow your two eyeballs to be opened and reorient yourself to the environment you are. After you finish accessing your records or whenever you're ready to end the meditation, gently open your eyes. Pay more attention to the details of the room you are in, as well as the sounds, the smells, and the feel of your environment. You can gently sit back up if you were lying down on the bed or any plane surface. You may decide to be standing or sit down for some moments if that's what you prefer.

{B}. Reflect on the experience after you finish your meditation. Take out a pen and paper and write down anything that you remember about the experience. What images did you see? Did you feel, smell, taste, or hear anything? Try and read your note so that you can get some useful tips through your meditation. Make sure you keep your note safe in order to go back to it later.

**POINT TO NOTE:** Be aware that some of the information you receive during your session may not make sense or seem meaningful. However, accessing your Akashic records often may help you to know the meaning of all the images you saw. This keeps becoming clearer and easier.

{C}. Repeat the process regularly to continue learning more. Make sure you engage your meditation as often as possible, like weekly or day to day interval. This helps you to get better understanding of your meditation. You may keep the same question every time, or come up with a new question if you are satisfied with what you got from your last session.

For instance, the moment you're confident that

you've learned everything you need to know about your past professions, you may move to the next stage by asking yourself questions relating to your past relationships.

The healing energy of the Akashic Records helps everybody to get full liberty to embrace grace in everything you do. This will eventually assist us to override any form of illusion that must have been created from any source. This happens to be the most powerful and interesting tools on this earth. It is available to us to help us remember our connection with our sources.

# 2 YOUR AKASHIC RECORD READER

Is it worth paying a premium for an Akashic Record Reading? Yes, but it depends on the reader. Possibly the reader is extraordinary and is using the "Akashic Record reading" specially as a justification for their prices. This type of reader is a much different breed, so to speak, than institutionally trained psychics. Some readers can identify discrepancies in your records versus your own soul's communication. Ideally, a reader can use meta-data and certain contextual information in your records to give you the information you might not even consider and that other reader would not see.

It is important to work with your own Akashic Record Keeper regularly.

Some people say that these records are automatically and continually updated; however, that has not been my experience. I notice that I have to consciously work with my Akashic Record keeper to make updates happen. I have observed this for many other people as well.

The book titled Akashic Records: Collective Keepers of Divine Expression, by Lumari is an interesting book to read. It is a channeled book. The author channels beings who claim to be the owners of the Akashic Record system. The book is short but weird in a good way. I found it interesting how craftily vague the writing is and how dichotomous it was in terms of blame and responsibility (and karma). This makes sense since information in the wrong hands creates terrible consequences and the beings in charge of such a system would be pretty stuck on, or obsessed with responsibility.

Although the book never comes out and says it directly, the Akashic Record system is, according to the book, essentially part of a different universe and the beings managing it are multi-dimensional aliens. It was also made to sound like the beings themselves contained the information within their own minds. Now combine this with the concept that this record system contains "every thought, action, word, emotion, and experience" and you have, essentially, a gigantic alien surveillance matrix.

Now that sounds much scarier than a "universal spiritual library." Call them beings of light and it all sounds much easier to digest and accept. I am not necessarily disputing what every author out there has said about this "wonderful library in the sky." I am simply inviting you to think for yourself.

I work with my own Akashic Record keeper semi-regularly. You can use it to help accomplish your goals and move forward in your life in a positive way that you would be unable to do otherwise. The

Akashic Record system has its place; it isn't the end-all or be-all of spiritual information access, but it is certainly important to know how to work with it. Think of it as a stepping stone to greater awareness and understanding of your psychic-self.

You must also consider that not everything in the spiritual realms is roses and daisies, even though most people marketing their services to you would have you believe that, because it is just, quite simply, more convenient and easier for everyone involved to make a sale happen; it's easier without flooding a customer with a thousand meandering doubts or inviting oneself – as a reader and business owner – to be accosted by a hundred tiny annoyances. Simple rosy stories make things easy, especially when it comes to something as complex and strange as the Akashic Records.

What does this mean for you? When it comes down to it: you have seniority. You are ultimately responsible for your life, decisions, karma, and spiritual experiences. It will certainly help to have the right tools to help you access, manage, and work with your spiritual information, but you are the final arbiter when it comes to how you decide to use that information.

It is up to you to investigate the Akashic Record space and discover what you can use, what to file away for later, when to update your inner space, etc.

The Akashic Records can be seen as another resource in your spiritual tool-box – one of many resources, ideally. If you fail to seek, you will fail to see. So far, it's in the unknown, you will need patience and understanding to tap into the realm. People without patience will keep wasting their precious time trying to seek their Akashic records because the Akashic readers do not respond to impatience. You must learn how to be calm and focused. People fail in life not because they've never tried, rather they've been trying in the wrong way. Way of approach is very crucial and if you aren't careful, you will lose direction. Therefore, stay determined to access your akashic records with your readers.

# 3 WORKING WITH YOUR AKASHIC RECORD KEEPER

It is pretty important to meet your Akashic Record Keeper and learn how to actually work with him/her. Akashic record keepers are significantly different in terms of the healing you receive when you work with them compared to other guides. It might be a bit more accurate to say that you receive an "update" from them rather than traditional healing, although the experience is definitely healing overall. You can look at what your record keeper does to your aura and inner space as something very similar to defragmenting your hard drive.

So, what does that mean exactly? Well, files on your computer are stored in discrete units called "blocks." Ideally, these blocks should be "contiguous," or in a big long chunk if the files are big. In the real world, what usually ends up happening is that files are not stored in this fashion, but get dispersed across the entire physical hard drive. The process of organizing those dispersed files into large continuous blocks is called "de-fragmenting."

Obviously, this is just a metaphor, but essentially, your Akashic record keeper does something similar with the sub-conscious energies, and images in your chakras and layers of the aura. Your record keeper makes related images in your aura contiguous across different layers; you can feel it too. This is how my record keeper explained it to me. The metaphor illustrates the process well because you actually feel much smoother after working with your Akashic record keeper.

However, your information about what your record keeper does may be different for you. Hence, it is wise to communicate with your guide and ask them to explain what they do specifically to your own space, rather than assume my answer applies to everyone.

It is also their job to help keep track of your pictures and various events over different lifetimes; therefore, learning how to work with this kind of spirit guide allows you to access your unique information on your past lives and deeper wisdom. It also allows you to have more control over what you create in your life. Do you really want to end that last relationship with your ex for good? You might start by having your Akashic Record Keeper update all the pictures in your space about that person and then bring that information into a present time vibration.

Want to see what you are capable of as a spirit? Look at categories of different past lives that vibrated really highly, like at a gold color, for example. It will give you insights on how to channel into the realm without delay.

This kind of access can be beautiful and wonderful

and, also, potentially very hazardous. Generally, it's fine to look at things if you're neutral, but you probably don't want to bring, or download, the information you aren't ready to handle – especially if there is a lot of karma involved. So, it is important to remember, realistically, how capable you are currently, and what you have time to deal with and explore.

What your record keeper looks like.

How it feels to work with your record keeper and what it is like.

How to access past life information that will benefit you in this lifetime.

What specific healing projects your record keeper can help you with today.

This class is short and sweet at 48 minutes in length and gives you exactly what you need to get started working with your Akashic Record Keeper.

However, people have varying levels of experience and some may prefer a longer recording, with a deeper introductory meditation. So, we have also included two additional recordings, including a clairvoyant meditation introduction and a one-hour meditation on opening, and clearing out the feet chakras. This powerful grounding workshop recording is normally only sold as part of a larger package. But we'll throw it in for free. You will receive the three recordings in an mp3 format, which can be played on any modern computer or listening device.

As a healer, it is very important for you to be able to say hello to not only your own record keeper but also other people's record keepers – especially for your clients. When you can say hello to a client's record keeper you can offer them a whole new level of resolution, spiritual healing, and transformative experience. The secret is direct and if strictly followed, you will always find it easy to connect soon, fast and convenient.

Knowing your Akashic Record Keeper and being in communication with her/him is necessary for every spiritual practitioner and meditator. They are a special spirit guide that you will work with for the rest of your life. Get introduced to him, or her, in this safe and supportive class recording by experienced teachers. They will guide you through difficult and powerful discoveries. They are the readers and keepers of your past, present, and future records. They understand the rudiments and possibility to make you understand fast and easily. Keep in touch because they would be helpful.

Once you've discovered your Akashic keeper, you can ask any questions you can think of. For instance, you can ask questions ranging from the past, present, to the future. This helps you to create solid awareness as fast as you can without spending too much of your time. Don't forget to always remain stable and never try to gamble.

# 4 AKASHIC READING ON INCLUSIONS

The people of this planet have used exclusion in so many, many differing ways in the past and now is such an appropriate time to look at this way of treating each other and your earth and allowing yourselves to change and to be bias towards inclusion rather than exclusion. Exclusion is whenever each of you choose to not make allowance for another's way of seeing life. If each of you were to write down in a day how often you exclude others, you may be surprised at how often this is.

This is every time you criticize another for their seemingly different ways of doing things. An example we will give you with our humor on this is the "toothpaste tube" - yes, we know that some of you simply do not care where you squeeze it and others can see that the tooth paste tube must be squeezed in a particular way. The one with the particular way is excluding the one who doesn't care. Why we see this with humor is that you could each have a toothpaste tube and then no one is then excluded.

There are often simple solutions to the traits and habits that humans acquire and that they use to exclude. If you take on our little exercise of writing down each time you exclude others in your day and then allow yourself to see where you could include people, you may be surprised at how easy this is to change.

If each of you reading this, were to do this you would be making a change, not only to your world but also to the whole of humanity. Does inclusion mean that you have to include every human being in everything that you do? The answer to this is 'no'. What inclusion means to humans on the planet at this time is that you observe your life, you look at how you, yourself include others:

Are you selective in that inclusion? Why do you select to include this one and not that one? As you question this in yourself, you will understand more of your bias's your judgments and why you have these biases and judgments. Inclusion means observing what is appropriate in a particular situation. When you observe appropriately, with integrity, you will find that sometimes it is not appropriate to include a particular person or group. This is OK - you have done your homework so to speak. You have made observations with integrity and then decided that at that particular moment it is not appropriate to include this person or this group.

From this time on, we would ask you to check on your own bias in a situation and question this bias with integrity and make any changes that you can that will serve inclusion. Inclusion will be a concept that you all as humans will hear more of as your world changes - your world can't continue to change unless you all choose inclusion more often.

## TRACING THE INSPIRATION

Inspiration is what brings new thoughts, new concepts and new inventions to your planet. When you say… "I had the inspiration to… "or "I feel inspired to…."What you are saying is that you had a connection with your intuitive process and that intuition sparked something that allowed your inspiration in that moment. It may be that you think that someone else gave you the inspiration because the words or concept was spoken or written by them.

What happens here is that you were choosing and allowing inspiration to come to you and as you made that choice, you heard or found the words or pictures or understanding that you required in that moment that took you to the place where you could see the possibility for your inspiration. So often you attribute your inspiration to someone or something else, when they were just part of the process that allowed your inspiration to come to the surface so that you could have greater awareness.

Inspiration is often us winking at you…. nudging you…. giving you a clue as to what could be beneficial to you in your current state or situation. Your choice is to have awareness of it, to allow it through and then take whatever it is to the fruition that you feel that you require with it.

Therefore, inspiration is part intuition, part awareness and part knowing what will help you next.

You can play more with inspiration.... ask for it...'What inspiration can you give me that will help me in this situation?' Then be open to what arrives, even if it doesn't come packaged how you thought it might.

Inspiration is a valuable concept to have..., play with yours so that you have the ability to increase your awareness of it.

## HOW TO ATTRACT CURIOSITY?

Curiosity is a wonderful ability for human beings to have. We encourage you to use your curiosity as it is an underdeveloped ability of many of you although in some of you it is what we would call overdeveloped.

How are you with curiosity?

The ease of information in the age that you live in has allowed some of you to use your curiosity to a greater extent than you require. You are always looking into and observing new and interesting things to you, information, processes and ways of being. With this some of you have come to be living your life outside of yourselves.....you want more and more information and do not always allow space for understanding and integration.....then you are on to the next topic, object or idea.

If this is you.... slow down and rather than taking on more and more.....take some time and space to just be, this will help you balance your internal and then your external journey. Be satisfied with less information and more feeling.... have a go at this and allow your curiosity to observe the difference that this can contribute to your life.

If you are one who has very little curiosity, you may find that if you choose to explore things further, to expand them out more, then you will come to a place where you can see how your life and living can change. That you are able to live a fuller life, being and doing what interests you most…..what you receive most of your enjoyment from and also this brings a different balance into your life.

Curiosity can often bring satisfaction as you explore parts of your life that you haven't yet allowed their fuller expansion, for example, joy, peace, and ease. You can understand more of you, of who you really are and what contribution that you have for yourself, your family, your friends, your workplace and humanity as a whole. As you choose to develop or re-balance your curiosity, we are watching and enjoying this aspect of you.

We use this to give you hints, to help you develop your intuitive process/recognition more and we also use your curiosity to allow synchronicities to come your way. Have more awareness of this…..connect the dots and use these moments of synchronicity to acknowledge that you have a beautiful connection with us and your connection is working well. Enjoy your balanced curiosity…..it's a fun part of your life and living. Start giving in Love through your curiosity!

## HOW CAN WE DO THIS MORE KEEPERS, LIVING MORE IN THIS NOW MOMENT?

Yes, such a challenge for human beings! Many of

you understand the concept of this in your mind…..that your past has gone, that your future has not yet arrived, so all that you have is this moment now. Where the challenge for you is, is bringing this concept into play in your living.

How is this done?

We will start by saying that you most likely be in the moment more than you 'think' that you do. So, if we have a look at those moments…..you may be chatting with friends or family and something very funny is said…..and what happens at that moment is that you laugh out loud…..spontaneously.

Laughing is one of those expressions that is very hard to do if you are not present now. Even if you are pretending to laugh, you have to be present with that pretense to allow the sounds and facial expressions of laughter to be expressed.

For many of you, you are on auto-pilot most of your time. Another aspect of this is that time doesn't exist…..it is just a concept humans use to live their lives with. We don't have time on our side.

In the newer energies, you are going to become more used to what is currently a concept to you, the concept of time not being so important to your lives…..you will come to understand other ways of living without time being what regulates your lives.

For now

It would benefit you to make a choice to be more present in your day. If you make this choice and give the intent to be present…..you may find that you enjoy your days more, you will enjoy them more because you have chosen to enjoy each moment.

That intent could be something like this…..when you wake in your morning, simply say with feeling to yourself 'I intend to be more present in my life this day.'

Then at the end of your day, without judgment of yourself, just remember those moments where you were fully in that moment, where you were fully present in your life. As your life goes on, if you make a choice for this, you will find that you have the opportunity to feel more fulfilment, contentment, ease, space and peace in your life.

The newer energies will support you in this. Understand Dear Ones, that although you have the opportunity and potential to be able to BE more PRESENT......while you are a human being it is not currently available to you to be like this 24/7. Just choose more presence for yourself and allow being present to be a gift for you.....a present for you :-) that will allow you more ease with living now

## HOW DOES IMAGINATION HELP US AND HOW CAN WE INCREASE OUR IMAGINATION?

If you each as human beings were to step into your imagination more, what wonderful living you would have now on your planet.

Mostly human beings think....

What if you were to imagine?

It is the human part of you that thinks and the being part of you that imagines. It seems so simple to us.... If you 'BE' more, you IMAGINE more.....you use your INTUITION more.....you feel more JOY.....you feel more GRACE.....you flow with more EASE.

As a human being would this add to your life, would this make your time on this planet more enjoyable? If you are to answer 'YES' to this, then we would say to you.... 'BE' more and with 'BEING' more, you allow your imagination to bring forth an energy that is helpful to you as the being that you are.


## HOW DO YOU 'BE' MORE?


Choosing to be in a place of nature more often will help this. Your own backyard, a park, a beach, a mountain, a river, a creek…..anywhere where you can have a space that allows you to breathe deeply, listen to the various sounds of nature…that allows you to see the wonder of nature and how it contributes to you.

If you are choosing this, then when you are just 'BEING' in nature with no human distractions…....that is when you can allow your imagination the freedom to express the energy that it is. This will be different for each of you. Making a choice for expression of your imagination will help you in so many ways.

In your allowing comes the synchronicities, the moments when you connect the dots, the moments or occasions when your awareness increases, either helped by yourself or us…It is usually prompted by us because you have asked and opened up to more of who you really are and more of what is available to you.

Would you enjoy this?

Is there a potential that more imagination in your

life could bring you more JOY in your life…..that your life could be fueled by that deep inner knowing that you have help 24/7 if you would slow and sometimes STOP your busyness and allow the space for it and welcome the help that is there for you? We say 'What a potential!

## HOW TO OVERCOME YOUR FEAR, EXPERIENCING ENERGY IN THIS CHANGING PLANET

Yes, many of you are experiencing what you call 'fear'.

The experience you are choosing as individuals and as well as a collective is because there is much change happening in your world currently and your perception of that change takes you to the state that you as humans call 'fear'.

Why do you go into fear?

You go into fear because of your expectations, you have lived in a world where change was slow…..you were able to cope with what was occurring. Now that your planet has shifted into a new way and you don't as yet have a clear perception of what this new way is… you go into fear as a way of coping with this.

This new way and the new humans are going to be so different to what you have been used to…..you won't be able to go backwards…..to go back to 'normal' to how you used to see things. This shift has taken away the possibility of that, so now it is time for you to allow you different ways of perceiving and doing and most of all being.

As human beings on this planet at this time, you are so used to planning ahead…..taking your perceived security from 'knowing' what is going to be next for you…..for today…..for tomorrow…..for next week…...for next month. Knowing that you had a 'plan' somehow allowed you to think that you had control over your life…..that you could cope with your life as long as your life mostly went to plan.

Now that has changed.

What you are moving towards is TRUST, just trusting that all is well as you bring your perceptions into a different place into a space of this moment. Even though you will still make plans…..it may not work if you choose to get on an airplane if you have not booked a ticket…..you will find that for your life to flow, you will be required to have flexibility about those plans…..some may see this as losing control.

What that flexibility will do is to allow you to be in this moment more…..to feel this moment more.

How this will help you will be that you will feel you more…..feel others more and feel your planet more. Your energy is changing…..others energies are changing and the energy of your planet is changing. Expect change…..be surprised and delighted with it and as you do this you move from fear towards TRUST. As you move towards trust, you allow synchronicities to flow to you. You allow solutions to situations that work out far better than you could imagine yourself. Then as you allow this into your life and living…..you also allow more EASE. Now…..what would you choose…..fear or ease? Embrace the changes that appear in your life and you will live with much more EASE. TRUST!

# 5 THE HUMAN NATURE AND BEHAVIORS

As a human being on this planet at this time, your possibilities are immense. Not only are they immense, but the possibility of the immenseness is also continually creating it is continually increasing. As a human being, you have chosen to only perceive some of your possibility only a small part of your possibility, even though your possibility has no limitations.

How do you do that?

You make choices for your life and living based on what you perceive you know. What you perceive you know is based on your expectations. Your expectations are based on what has gone before…

What you were taught.
What you grew up with.
What your culture tells you.

What your country tells you.
What your family tells you.
What your parents tell you.

As you are able to change any of these perceptions of expectations then you are able to open yourself up to increasing possibilities. For some of you, depending on the current age of your body, you have grown up with very different concepts of technology and what technology can do for you as well as your fears or joy in using technology.

If you were to go back even a couple of generations in your family you could see that the expectations around technology were so different from the possibilities that are available now. So, we say to you, be ready for it drop your expectations and open yourself up to the amazing, increasing and at this moment unimaginable possibilities that are coming your way.

You as new humans in a new time on your planet will look back on this time as being so limited, so full of expectations that were bound or given boundaries by how the human mind is now and not by the unlimited possibilities available to you.

Are you going to make a choice now to drop your expectations and open yourself up to the limitless possibilities that are increasingly and sometimes daily coming into your existence? Here is a question for each day. "What possibilities are available for me today?" And enjoy your amazement at the synchronicity that occurs.

## HOW TO CREATE AWARENESS ON OUR TOLERANCE IN OUR DAILY LIVES

Your increased Tolerance of yourselves and each other is a key in having more peace on your earth, and you all know this. It really comes back to you giving yourself and others much more allowance, much more accommodation than you do now. How often each day do you make a judgment about yourself that judges you to not 'make it', to not shape up how your mind 'thinks' that you 'should'? It is now time to change this to make allowances for you that allows you to feel you as you really are. We can say to you in this instance that you are Divine and Magnificent being having a human experience and that is a deep truth. You can read these words, skim over these words and nothing changes.

So, we would like to say this again to you. You are dearly and deeply loved by us as you are a piece and a part of our family…..we are Divine and Magnificent and as you are a piece and a part of us, you are a part of our family and so you are Divine and Magnificent as well.

You cannot be!

Now take a deep breath… and another and STOP and allow you to feel this… Choose to do this now and feel our family essence. At this moment feel your tolerance for you, just feel it… nothing else matters just now except that you are feeling you and feeling your own Magnificence. While you are in this space, you know that all is well with you; you just 'know' this. Hold this essence of you for as long as you can. When you are in this space, this essence of you and you are being tolerant of you, then you allow you more tolerance of those around you.

This is how you change your world and the world around you. If you were to choose tolerance of you for the rest of your day and for your next day, you are contributing to more peace in your life and on your earth. Maybe no one notices what you are doing, maybe no one comments, does it matter if you feel different, if you feel softer if you are feeling more of you?

## KNOWING YOUR EXPECTATIONS AS HUMANS

The expectations that humans place on themselves need to be questioned. How often have you placed an expectation on yourself that you haven't met? This may be something practical like.... 'I will exercise every day.' It may be something you think about yourself, 'I am never going to be good enough for God.'

If you were to list your expectations, you may find that your list is long, longer than you expected. You make a choice for each one of these expectations because you decide that or you allow others expectations of you to become what your criteria for your life are or should be or could be.

If you were to take the expectation that is the most in your mind.... the one that you think about the most, that you haven't met, now have a good look at it:

Is this your expectation of you?
Is this another expectation of you?

Is this what you would really choose for you?
Would choosing this for you bring you joy, bring you ease?
If the expectation would bring you joy and ease, then what is stopping you?
What thoughts or actions are stopping you from taking this expectation to fruition?

If the expectation belongs to another human being or if the expectation is not what you would choose for you…. then just drop it…. just allow it to disappear from your life, and then feel the EASE and JOY that is available to you because you allowed YOU to make a choice for YOU.
Today would be a good day to do this.

## HOW TO LIGHT UP AS KEEPERS

We share with ourselves, insights on how powerful lighting up our minds through our keepers. This will give you some understanding about 'lightness'. It has been usual for human beings in their past times to have heaviness about them and their way of being. This heaviness has come from how each individual human has judged themselves in almost all aspects of their lives. When individual judgment creates energy of heaviness, then how can the whole of humanity feel light?

As you are all entangled with each other you often feed on each other's heaviness. This heaviness may come from how you as individuals and groups and as a whole think about a particular subject or issue. You may agree or disagree to varying degrees about a particular issue and as you think and voice your opinion or take action or react in any way about this, you often then hold the energy around this in a heavy vibration. The heavier the vibration the more challenging it is for humanity to 'lighten up'.

There may be a situation in your world that affects many of you. So, you each express your viewpoint about this. Often this viewpoint comes from fear, fear of what has happened, what could happen or what you have convinced yourself will happen.

There is another way, what if you were to have an observation that this particular event has occurred and then every time this comes into your mind, into your conversation, you allow yourself a different perception? Could you as an individual allow some heaviness to dissipate which would then allow some lightness in by you changing your thoughts, words, actions and reactions?

Yes, you can.

As each of you choose differently.... in other words, choose love rather than fear, then you allow more lightness into your personal world as well as into the energy of the whole of humanity.

Could you do this?

Would you do this next time a situation arises? If you are able to choose lightness and love over fear and heaviness, then you have made a contribution to the whole of humanity. If you are able to make changes to your habits, you are then allowing the space for others to make changes to their habits.

You will feel lighter and they also have the potential to feel lighter. Your lightness will allow more ease into your moments, your days and your life. Can you choose lightness in this moment?

## HOW TO LOVE OURSELVES MORE

It is time now for human beings to make more choices to love themselves more and more. This seems so simple when you as humans read these words and we in spirit know that you have so much difficulty with this. You may want to say, "Well yes, I know that. I know that me loving myself helps all other areas of my life to flow. I also think that I do love myself." And we in spirit will say to you, there's more, there is much more, so much more that in your current energies on your planet you are only just beginning to understand this. If you were able to see your colors, your sounds, your magnificence, you would be in such wonderment that this is you.

If you were to look back on the last 10 years of your life in the perspective of you loving you, what has changed? Do you love you more? Do you see more of your magnificence than you did before this time? Or have you made a choice to release one set of 'rules' of how you can be in this world and just changed them for another set of 'rules' without allowing any more of yourself love to open up to you?

Now is the time when you are being supported by us to change this. It is time for you to release your self-imposed 'rules', ideas and concepts about 'how' and 'how much' you can be loved by you. We will talk to you of how we love you… Each and every one of you all is loved by us with absolutely no exceptions.

There are no conditions on our love. Our love is unconditional. It does not matter what you have done, what you think, how you have portrayed yourself on this planet...you are loved by us unconditionally. It does not matter what others 'think' of you or what you 'think' that others think of you, you are loved unconditionally by us. It does not matter what you have done in what you call your "past lives" or what you may do in any future life...you are loved unconditionally by us. Feel this, take a deep breath or two now and feel this love in your heart center now.

If you have taken yourself out of your mind place to stop and feel this love that we have for you, you will know how you can bring yourself into the space of self-love that will serve you in your daily life. It only takes a few moments of your time for you to -

Stop ---> Breathe ---> and feel us.

You will know when you make this connection as your whole energy will soften and, in this softening, you will feel the divine feminine energy within you... the soft warm nurturing mother energy. This is self-love. How many moments in your day can you allow you to come into and be in the love that is in this space for you?

If you choose to do this often in your day, you will allow your love for yourself to expand. As your love for you, your self-love expands, then you will become aware of how you make different choices than you did before and that these different choices, made from your space of self-love have the capacity to make changes in your life. What if you were to choose self-love as your first priority in your life? Could you expand with the choices that this gifts you? Self-love has the most expansive potential for self-change.

## WHAT HONESTY MEANS FOR HUMAN BEINGS AT THIS TIME ON PLANET EARTH

Honesty is about the breaking down of the parameters by which many of you have been living. You have chosen to believe and live by what others have told you or perceptions you have gained by observing others.
What if none of this was true for you?
What if your way of honesty is quite different to this?
You could ask:
How can I make it different?
How can I do honesty my way?

Honesty is really about your questioning. It's about you questioning you not others.....about how you perceive, feel and 'know' yourself. Pick a topic that is often in your mind, something that you sometimes puzzle over, that you aren't sure of and write it down if you care to, or just find some uninterrupted space and sit quietly.
Ask yourself questions about this topic:

Why do I believe this about this topic?
Who said that this is so for me?
Do I really agree with the general consensus on this topic?
What is it that feels true for me?

What if what feels true for me is totally different from the general consensus?
Does that matter to me, do I care?
If you find that it does matter and you do care, ask yourself, why?

Self-honesty is about you questioning you, not about you doing the 'right thing'.
More questions:

What is the 'right thing' in any particular situation?
Who says that it is the right thing?

When you come to a deeper space of self-honesty in you, you will also acknowledge and have some understanding in yourself that your Honesty with you is really all that matters to you. There are layers and layers of what humans call honesty. You come to your center, your core will help you understand for yourself what you perceive is honesty in any particular situation in your life. When you have found what you feel is an honest space for you, what is true for you… know that you always have the opportunity to go deeper.

Self-honesty is always about you questioning you and you may acknowledge that you don't have the answers just now. If you are into the 'rightness' or 'wrongness' of the topic or situation, then we would suggest to you that you stop and take a few moments to ask yourself questions. "Rightness and wrongness" is not about honesty, it is about judgment. Self-honesty is about you choosing for you and that is a gift that is available to everyone on this planet. What are you choosing now, honesty or dishonesty?

## EMBRACING COMPASSION THROUGH YOUR AKASHIC RECORDS

Compassion is a word that you all will hear more often from now on. This is because compassion is an energy that is so powerful, whether used by an individual or used by many. Like when there is a natural occurrence happening on your planet, for example, the Japanese tsunami in the year 2011.

This was Gaia making the shifts and changes she needed to make to accommodate the new energies. When you are able to understand that this was a necessary part of your evolution, you will be able to see this occurrence with compassion. Compassion was the gift that all of those who made their transition, gave you. This was an opportunity on a global scale for you all to feel your compassion.

Compassion is an attribute that is allowing the vibrations on your planet and in your own energy field to change, to move towards the light. Many of you are embracing this, embracing these changes and as you do, you move away from human drama and fear. How light does that feel for you?

Just stop for a moment now, and feel this. Feel your compassion for yourself as you have allowed yourself to make and accept this change in you. As you choose compassion, you allow others to see how it is, to feel how it is and this is making a difference on this planet at this time.

How can you be more compassionate in your daily lives?
Ask yourself when you are in a situation of drama:

Does this really matter? ...Could I just smile and allow the other human being to be and do what they feel is appropriate at this time and not agree or disagree - just simply 'be' with whatever the situation is?
Just know that all is well and that you are in that place at that time to increase your understanding of compassion.
How does this feel to you?
Does this feel that you are lighter?

That is all you are required to be - to be a light worker in these situations, to carry the light, to allow the light that you have inside to show, to be seen by others. How do you think you can tap into this amazing power of deep compassion in your Akashic Records? It all starts with your true nature and inner man conscious.

## AN OPPORTUNITY FOR CHANGE

Many have wondered what these next years would bring for themselves. There have been all sorts of predictions and each of you has the choice as to what you believe about these predictions. I will suggest you believe the predictions that are grounded in love. How we see these next years, are that they will give humanity more opportunity for change.
Many fear, "change" without actually having a

close look at what that change may involve for them. Are you one of these or do you embrace change with a sense of adventure, with a curiosity of what is new, what can you see or do next that will delight you and bring joy? Of course, our suggestion for you for these coming years are to take out your sense of adventure - dust it off and pursue the opportunities that become available to you as your years' progress.

There will be much more opportunity for change available. This may mean to you as humans, a change in the way you think about a concept or idea, a change in how you approach something that has been in your life for some time, or it could mean that you will be given the gift of many changes this coming year that will make great changes in your life.

Ask yourself, "Am I ready to embrace the changes that come my way?" If you are able to embrace the changes available to you specifically - we say to you to do this with an awareness of curiosity and bring your sense of adventure into play. This will bring the changes into your life with ease.

Change is not required to be 'hard' - change is often required in your individual lives to bring you ease and with this ease, if you make a choice for ease then you can have the feeling of joy. The feeling of joy is depleted in most human lives. Would you choose more joy for yourself?

Therefore, you can make a choice to take the opportunities that present themselves through these next years, to embrace any changes that come your way and allow them into your life with as much ease as you can. This will allow you to have a different life. These times allow you the opportunity and potential for JOY in your life. An opportunity that will make a great impact in your life is the one you are willing to embrace. Tap into your Akashic records to know your best opportunity!

# 6 ATTAINING CLARITY IN OUR PERCEPTIONS AND OUR SPIRITUAL JOURNEY

Clarity is the clearness with which you each as individuals perceive your journey. There will be moments for each of you that are so clear and you know that you are in clarity about that particular situation or instance on your journey.

Then there are the other times…and for some of you, this is most of the time that you feel so unclear. For you to have clarity about a particular situation, you may need some quiet time to be able to perceive and articulate what it is that you would like to have clarity on, that you would like to be clearer about.

Often you ask for clarity but you do not want to change anything or you do not have simple clear questions to ask. It can be like a muddy puddle and you skirt around the edges without jumping into the puddle to really see what needs to be addressed...does this sound familiar? What would help you when you are making a choice for clarity around a particular issue or situation is that you take a pen and paper and write down all that you currently perceive about the situation. You may make headings like...

What is good?
What I like about this situation.
What needs attention or needs to be addressed about this situation.

Then write down all that you know - this will help the situation to become clearer in your mind and you need to have a clearer mind so that you can then articulate simple clear questions to us. You may also like to write down any possible solutions or part solutions that come to your awareness. When you have done this, take some quiet, alone time and tune in to us as your guides, helpers, angels, higher self or whatever it is that you prefer to call us. Then just sit with your pen and paper and ask your questions.
The answers will vary for all of you even if you ask the same question at the same time...except that what you could receive could be different. This is because you are all different, with different experiences this lifetime and in those lifetimes that you perceive have gone before this one. There would also be differing attitudes about being able to receive communication from us. Some of you will 'see', some of you will 'hear' and some of you will 'know' and there may be a combination of these abilities as well. So, as you tune in you might like to write down anything that comes...do not

discount anything.

We often communicate to you in metaphors - there are so many ways we communicate to you. If you see a tea cup…write it down…just write down anything that comes to your awareness. When you are done, put your notes aside and then some hours later or even a day or so later take up your notes and see what you have written. We will take the teacup as an example…then simply write down what a teacup means to you;

Do you enjoy drinking out of a delicate teacup or do you prefer a mug? Do you like tea or not… what sort are your favorites? What does enjoying having a cup of tea feel like to you…..comfort, time for you or nurturing…..explore this. Ask any questions of yourself that come to your awareness and then, when you are finished, put your writings aside for a while…..maybe have a cuppa [smile] and then go back to your writings and read it and allow the clarity to come to you.

For some of you, you may not need to go through all of this process to allow your clarity to come into your awareness as you tune into us the clarity may be there. This is only one way to gain clarity - you will find a way that suits you. Some may find that by becoming clear in the question….the clarity comes.

Some may find that they will write down the question and then in the shower, or on their morning walk, the clarity comes. Each of you is different. Some of you may go through this process and still feel that you do not have clarity and there are some of you who will ask for clarity but not really want to choose the answer that clarity can give you. Are you allowing your heart to show you the answer, or are you giving your head a free rein to control the situation?

Clarity is knowing, it is you knowing what is going to serve you well. What is for your highest good at that time? Choosing to follow that clarity is another part of the process. Not all of you will choose to do this and that is where your free choice and free will comes in and we have the greatest respect for you in this.

If you do not choose to follow the path of your clarity, we will be with you when you again ask the same question…and with humor we say…there may or may not be a different answer. If you are to ask for clarity, receive the gift of clarity, choose to follow the clarity that you have gained, then you will find that there will be more flow and ease to your situation. Trust comes into this…you have trusted yourself and trust has allowed you clarity. Can you trust? Can you trust yourself for your own knowing and awareness? It's time you gave it a try.

## FOLLOWING YOUR ENERGY

The simplest way to explain this is to give them an understanding of their own intuitive processes and then show them how they use their intuitive processes to 'follow the energy'. The first step in following the energy is to be able to know how your own intuitive process works. Ask the person to bring to mind a time when they knew that they used their intuition. Ask them to recognize that they got the intuitive thoughts, words or pictures. They then used these thoughts words or pictures to take some form of action which was applicable to the situation - how did this result?

When they took that action…that was them 'following the energy'. How did they know that they were 'following the energy'? If a person can understand this process, then they understand their intuition and following the energy is actually following their intuition, regardless of what their mind is thinking. If they are unsure, they may like to write down a few instances of them following the energy and just be aware of how it goes. Ways to know if you are 'following the energy' is when everything flows, when it all goes well without much effort on your part. Following the energy is simply following your intuition without questioning it.

## BEING YOUR FULL SELF AND HOW THIS PLAYS OUT IN YOUR LIVES

The human being has developed over their time to this stage in their evolvement where their curiosity about themselves continually has them in question about themselves, as individuals and about the whole of humanity. This we see as wonderful from our side of the veil and we encourage questions as to when we are asked to give you information about yourselves, your understanding takes you closer to peace on earth.
As each of you are in the space of your full self- more and more, then each of you individually is asking for and receiving more peace in yourselves and this contributes to peace on earth. Yes, we do see that peace on earth is now a possibility and we are joyful to help any human that chooses peace at any moment of their lives.

Being your full self is choosing peace. So, how does this actually play out in your daily lives? We will explain it this way; in each moment of your life, you have a choice for peace. If today you actually chose to spend one hour of your day in peace and your friend also chose to spend one hour today in peace, then that would be two hours of peace that add up towards peace for the earth, peace for your world.

While you are in this space of peace you are being your full self as a human being. This one hour today of peace may not sound to you like a lot but if many of you chose this it adds up and in that adding up it allows more of you to see and observe what it is to have and be peace on earth. When you as an individual are in this state of peace, you are able to be rather than do - to feel joy - to contribute - to receive - to use your gifts to their fullest capacity, of this and more allows you ease and as you receive that ease you are being your full self. It is like it goes around in a circle; as you use your gifts and feel your joy, you can receive, you can contribute and you feel ease.

Feel the ease and you feel joy and peace, you can contribute and receive and this allows your gifts to come easily. So, one engenders the other and they all are part of your full self. When you bring your full self into any situation or relationship, you also bring all of these other gifts with you so this allows your expression and expansion and then doing this allows others to see and understand and use their own expression and expansion. And so around and around the circle goes and all of this will contribute to peace on your earth.

## ALLEVIATING OUR CONCERNS ABOUT MONEY

Because humans have made money their way of exchange, humans now often perceive that there is never enough money to exchange for the goods and services that they perceive that they require. Many humans feel that there is more money outgoing than incoming and this creates a discrepancy in their lives that concerns them and does not allow them to have a joy.

So, what to do about this? It is all about your perceptions of money. In this world at this time, money or the lack of it is high on many peoples' list of what stresses them the most. Would it be possible for humans to change their perceptions about money, about how they use it and how they can make different choices?

Each and every human has different perceptions about money, from not caring about it to making it the most important thing in their lives with most people being somewhere in between these 2 opposites. If we consider that money is a form of energy that is to be used to help us live our lives then why do we allow the perceived lack of it to often take over our lives and be the criteria by which we make decisions about our lives?

Would it be possible for us as humans to choose joy as the criteria by which we make decisions about our lives and how we live our lives? If each human was able to swap money for the joy they currently have in their lives, they would often find that they have more money than joy. If a human was able to actually feel increasing amounts of joy and chose to be able to feel joy as the criteria for making decisions in their lives, then would their lives change?

We would say that if a human could do this, use joy as the criteria for making decisions for their life, then this world would be a different place, more love would show up and more peace would show up. Choosing money as a reason for making decisions will not bring you joy, love or peace.

What would you like? Money or Joy?

Could you change your choices and when you have your next decision to make, could you decide that you would make the choice that gave you the most joy - how would you feel? And how would you feel if you made your next decision based on money - how would you feel? We suggest that before each decision concerning money, you ask yourself, 'Would this decision give me the most joy?'

If you were to make this a habit even for 3 months, you may be surprised at the differences in your life. We are talking about all decisions concerning money from buying a chocolate bar to buying a car or a house and all other decisions in between. When you are able to be more discerning in your choices about joy and money, you may be surprised after 3 months how you perceive money and for some of you, you may even get to the stage of having money that you don't feel compelled to go out and spend.

Spending - can you spend that money and still have that money? So, as you question your every and actual spending decisions with... 'Will this give me joy?' You may choose joy rather than spending and then by making that choice over and over again you may then 'have money' or be in an improved financial position.

When your concerns about money have been

alleviated somewhat and as the joy is building in your life, you may find that you can rely on your feelings of joy to keep you contented, peaceful and able to love yourself and others more, rather than on the goods and services that you used to choose instead of joy.

We ask you if you are reading this because you have concerns about money to consider using this simple question; 'Will this give me joy?' for at least 3 months and see how you feel in 3 months' time. It may help you to write down how you feel about money now and then, in 3 months, how you feel then as you just may be surprised at the difference. Joy is that feeling of peace and love that allows you to 'know' that all is well with you.

## THE REASON WHY HUMANS CANNOT SUSTAIN THEIR CURRENT LEVELS OF ANGER

These current levels of anger will not sustain in the new energies as there will be no support for them. Humans themselves will not accommodate other humans feeling high levels of anger. Angry humans will be shown that there are other avenues or ways that they can address their anger.

This will be done with love and the humans that have anger will no longer be able to sustain their current levels. This dissipation of anger will take place as a seemingly natural occurrence as more and more humans step into love. The more humans that step into love as a way of being, as an answer to or a solution to their current human situations the less that anger will be able to be sustained in the human psyche.

The energy of love is so much stronger, more vibrant and more active than anger so that the fear that is anger in any individual human will gradually fade. This will not be an instant solution although it could be as humans choose to make different choices than they have in their past.

An angry human is a human that holds fear dearer than love and allows small frustrations to build into larger situations. As they feel that they are losing control, losing control of the particular situation, losing control of their life and losing control of themselves…this is projected outwards.

The only solution to this is love - and love that is able to be embraced in a particular situation will help to diffuse and dissipate the anger. Even if this anger has been with this human for all or most of this lifetime, or it may be a continuance from another lifetime or lifetimes, it can be diffused with love if the human chooses.

Does a smile engender anger?

Is it possible for a human to smile and be angry at the same moment?

A smile allows the body to relax and for the heart to show its love and of course, a hug can help a lot as well. A simple touch with almost no words can help anger to dissipate, to dissolve. When next you are in a situation where another human is angry, allow your heart to soften, allow the anger to be theirs, not yours and be aware of how your body is reacting. When you are feeling love for the person, your body cannot react in anger.

So, if one of you remembers love then the anger will not be as intense and you are moving out of your fear and towards love. This is what we ask you to do when you are in the midst of anger -

remember your love - you will be helping yourself, the human who is in anger and humanity. Anger takes many forms from road rage to physical attacks and holding love in your heart is the answer.

## WHY ARE HUMANS ALWAYS TRYING TO ATTAIN THEIR PERCEPTION OF A HIGHER LEVEL OF AFFLUENCE

The human experience allows each human to see what else is available to them and to think that this is what they would like to attain. They think that their life and their life's experiences will improve for them when they attain this next or higher level. This may not actually be a higher level. It just may be a different place, space or experience to what they are having now.

Humans are always searching, searching, searching and the searching that they do on the outside of themselves and in the material, world leads them to think that being financially richer, more affluent, having more possessions or money is the way to go, the way to achieve a more contented space within themselves.

Now, more than ever before humans are questioning this concept that they have chosen as this concept is not actually delivering to them what they thought it should. You may say 'Okay Keepers, we understand that and we would say to you then why do you continue to search on the outside of yourselves?

Have you ever found joy outside yourself?
Have you ever found peace outside yourself?
Have you ever found love outside yourself?
If you are not able to find these energies inside yourself then, how do you expect to find them in the outside of yourself?

You have choices about what you allow to develop on the inside of you. You have choices about how much you allow this to expand to your outer being to be observed and seen by all who come in contact with you. These feelings of love, joy, peace are the most sustaining energies you can choose in this world.

These energies will sustain you in all areas of your life and in all your life's experiences. How is this so? If each human feel love, making all choices in love, then the choices and decisions made are made differently to those made without love and exactly the same applies to joy and peace.

Choices and decisions made with joy and peace allow the individual human to be able to live their life in the richness of their internal parameters. This allows them a life not influenced by external choices and desires of others. This is what we call a rich life, an affluent life, one in which the choices are made with love, joy and peace.

This does not mean that you don't have material things or that you don't choose quality material possessions. It just means that you make a choice for these items from YOUR internal parameters, not someone else's. Others will make their choices and decisions according to their beliefs and their life's experiences and that is ok for them. If you choose to have something different in your life, if this area of your life is of concern to you, then we say, look internally to make your choices and decisions and ask:

Will this give me joy?
Will this give me peace?
Will this give me love?

If you can answer 'yes' to any particular choice or decision and you continue to ask these questions for three months of your life, and then observe… have you felt more peace, more joy, more love?
This exercise can help you to change your habits and you can become more aware of how you really feel inside yourself and to question why you made decisions for you that were based on outside parameters. This is about you understanding you more fully.

# 7 AKASHIC RECORDS ABOUT HUMAN SUCCESS AND THEIR FEAR

Success is a complex process set up by humans to judge humans. To judge who they are, what they do, whom they have become and why they do what they do. As a process of human judgment, success does not serve humans well. It engenders fear and forestalls possibilities and potentials of humanity. In human terms, if you are successful, then that is to be applauded and encouraged and it is often not taken into account how this success was achieved - if it was achieved with love, with joy, with fun?

Success in spirit allows the deepening of feeling in humanity. This deepening of feeling is now an opportunity available to humanity through embracing the divine feminine, the love, the softness, the gentleness and the sharing of these with other humans. This allows all humans to be successful in feeling joy and joy is part of each human's purpose at this time.

Imagine that each moment of joy felt is a success

for the human feeling this joy and adds to the joy felt by other humans, which allows expansion and the embracing of who you really are. This is how we in Spirit see success. Worldly possessions and status do not have any impact on how we see success. These two attributes that the human race has invented have increased the fear for humans as individual humans compare themselves with each other. This comparison no longer has any value to humans or humanity as a whole.

As humanity progressed through the ages the number of reasons in humanity's thinking of ways to fear increased to the point where some actually feared fear. This is changing as there are no humans on the planet who have come to hold the fear for humanity and as humanity allows these 'fear holder humans' to take on or take away their individual fears, then humanity is finding a pathway which leads towards love and away from fear. This does not mean that the individual humans who are here on the planet at this time to hold the fear for humanity are fearful people themselves.

This means that those individuals have learned through their own experiences in this and other lifetimes what exactly fear is and they then, each in their own way, show others another way to perceive fear which allows for the decreasing of the fear energy on the planet. Since the (so-called by humans) natural disasters, that have been frequently news on the planet in the last few years, have been occurring the fear that these engendered in the past now turns more quickly in humanity from fear to compassion as those not involved in these situations feel compassion more quickly now than they did in the past. The time frame for each individual human to go from fear, on hearing the news, to compassion has lessened and this has served humanity well in these new energies.

Fear itself is imagined the energy in each individuals mind and can be built upon or dissipated at will. It is a situation of free will and if a human chooses with their free will to feel the fear and to stay in the human energy of the fear then that is their choice and we are in allowance of this.

Of course, we would encourage each of you to recognize the physical feelings, sensations and changes in how your own body reacts to fear. When each of you becomes aware of your own body reactions then you can start to address how you are about fear in yourself.

As you notice a particular sensation, like for instance you may get what humans call 'butterflies in your stomach' or it could be an ache or a pain in a particular part of your body, then you can start to address your fears. So, in the particular moment, you feel 'butterflies in your stomach' this is a signal that you have gone into fear mode. We ask you at this point to stop what you are doing – to take yourself to a quiet space where you can pay attention to your thoughts and take your thoughts back to what you were thinking when you first noticed this physical feeling of 'butterflies in your stomach'.

As you take your thoughts back and you come to a thought that for instance says 'I don't have enough money to pay the rent' or 'I'm concerned about whether my child is on drugs' we say to you have a notebook and write this down. Write down the date and time as well.

Then every time your butterflies arrive for a visit to your stomach, we say do this little exercise. When you have done this a number of times over a few weeks, have a look at what you have written in your notebook and then take the fear thought that is most prevalent for you, like 'I don't have enough money to pay the rent' or 'I'm concerned about whether my child is on drugs' and do this exercise: Take a sheet of paper and a pen - for those of you who understand the term 'mind map' we are going to do a mind map.

Draw a circle in the middle of the page and write your fear in the circle. Next, think of the worst thing that can happen if you 'didn't have enough money to pay the rent' (i.e. insert your particular fear) – draw a line out from your circle and write this possible consequence in the circle. Repeat this part of the exercise until you run out of fears about your issue. When you have completed this we ask you to set this aside for some hours or days – at least half a day and just go about your life.

After your 'set aside time' go back to your page and allow yourself to take each of the stories that you have written in each circle and ask yourself these questions:

Would this really happen?
What is the likelihood of this happening?
What can I do about this?
How soon can I take this action?
How do I really feel about this?
Why am I fearing this?
Why do I take myself through this perception of fear rather than having an understanding that I have the situation in my life at this moment that I would rather not have, and that it is within my own power to change it?

All that is required of me is to make different

choices. I know I can make different choices about taking myself through the process of fear and about making different choices for my life that will also eliminate the particular situation as well.

While this process of elimination of fear seems like a long one on paper, it will actually only take you a short time and the feeling of ease and freedom that comes with this exercise every time you practice it will feel like you have done so little but accomplished so much as it will become easier every time that you do it and eventually you will no longer require of yourself to write it all down.

You will be able to take yourself through the exercise quite quickly in your mind and best of all, you will find that fear no longer cripples you or your thinking in your life. So, we now remind you again that as you step away from fear you step towards love and this can change your life. What are you going to do about this in your life?

## HOW TO USE SIMPLICITY MORE IN OUR LIVES

Simplicity is a word not spoken about or used enough in human lives. Simplicity has the essence of the divine as it is a divine action.

If simplicity was used more in your complex world then there would be so much ease, so much freeing up of energies that are now employed in making your lives more complex. There is no requirement for humans to be complex or to make their lives complex.

In the divineness of human lives, there is a requirement for simplicity. It is a divine essence that, when applied in any situation, will bring on ease, a freedom that allows humans and therefore humanity a movement that will take them into the new energies.

How do humans embrace this (seemingly elusive to humans) action called simplicity?

Simplicity comes when each individual person challenges their own thinking and the ways that they apply their thinking. Simplicity is in your thinking first before it is in your doing.

To allow simplicity into your thinking, take something in your life that you find a challenge. Can you see the complexity in this matter? So, if you were to break this challenge up into a number of parts – get a pen and paper and do this now – break your challenge into about five parts. When you have done this, take the first part and have a really good look at it.

If this first part were all you have to contend with – all you have to do – all you have to think about, ask yourself:

Would you be able to take some action?
Would you be able to take some action today?
What is stopping you?
So, when you have finished reading this, ask yourself 'Am I going to do this now?'

Can you see that if you were to do this with each of the parts of your challenge that you presently have, your whole, as you perceive it, 'challenge' would allow you some ease? If you were to make a habit of this exercise then you would be taking some practical steps to add the gift of simplicity to your life.

Another way to see simplicity is that simplicity can

be a smile; it can be eye contact with feeling; it can be watching the sunrise or sunset, a walk-in nature or a quiet hour or two to yourself. Simplicity can be included in your life in many ways and if it is an easier or freer life that you would like or love then we say to you to bring an awareness of simplicity into the being and doing of your life.

Simplicity can also engender relationships between people. When simplicity is invested into interpersonal relationships this allows each individual a deepening of their spiritual attributes and as this occurs then the expression of each person's natural gifts and abilities can be allowed to shine, to come forward, to be appreciated and to allow more creativenesses in each human and also in those around them.

Simplicity is love in action. Love for yourself allows more love in your relationships, your work and in every part of your life. Is this what you would choose for yourself? Simplicity allows each human expansion – expansion of themselves as an individual to be energetically aligned with who they really are, to their fullest self-possible in the moment of simplicity.

## KNOWING THE POWER OF WISDOM AND HOW TO USE IT

Wisdom is love. Wisdom is the understanding that everything in this universe is love, that love permeates everything - every person, every place, every situation - that all there is love. It may not feel or look like this to a human that everything is love. We as your keepers can see the love in everything and as each of you gain more and more wisdom, you will have the gift of being able to see the love in people, places and situations where it would appear to some humans that there is no love or very little love.

The one who is able to see the love in everything is wise, has wisdom and this wisdom often comes from many lifetimes lived, from being an older soul and from the awareness of what love is and how it can be seen and used in everything.

Wisdom can come from saying something appropriate in any situation. It can also come from saying nothing and observing what is happening.

Wisdom can be a hug, a smile, a nod of the head to encourage another. It is both spoken and unspoken, it is both seen and unseen, and it is both felt and not felt. The wisdom can be felt by the person using it and not felt by the other person in the situation. Wisdom is knowing - just knowing that you 'know.'

Wisdom is trusting - just trusting that all is as it is.

Wisdom is allowing timing to take its place in everything.

Wisdom is being and not doing in particular circumstances.

Wisdom is allowing - allowing others to walk their own pathways, through their own challenges.

Wisdom is complete when it is used in the allowance of love.

Wisdom is for knowing, for receiving and available to those who recognize it.

The depth of wisdom is immeasurable to humans. As a human, you find it a challenge to comprehend the depth of wisdom. If you can just allow your wisdom to be love, you will have given a gift to yourself and humanity.

## HOW CAN WE EXPRESS OUR APPRECIATION AND GRATITUDE TO SPIRIT

The information for this seems easy to us in spirit although we know that you as humans may not see this.

When you communicate with us in whatever form it takes, whether directly or through a channel, we give you information. Some of you take this information and act on it.

Some of you act on part of it. Some of you simply keep asking more questions and take no or very little action. To the group that takes the information, allows it to permeate themselves as a human and then expands and expresses themselves with this allowance, we say to you that your expression and expansion is your appreciation. That is simply the way of communication between us.

To the ones who act on part of the information, we ask you to check with yourselves why you have a resistance to all of the information. With this we are not saying to you that you are required to act on all of the information - you all have free will. We are simply saying to you, have you missed anything that would be helpful to you, that may bring more ease into your life?

To those of you that take no or almost no action and ask more questions, we would say to you to have a look at 'change'. How are you with the change in your life and what can you do to allow more flexibility and acceptance of the change to come into your lives.

While we have given you some more information that will allow you to understand yourselves more, your appreciation comes to us simply by choosing to allow us in your lives, to guide you, to help you with your understanding of living a human life. We really appreciate you all for choosing to be humans, choosing to take on this human experience to come together as one and work towards peace on your earth. It is us who sit in wonderment of all your choices and human conditions that you have taken on to allow humanity to get to the place it is in now and to the potentials of where humanity is going towards.

## ENGAGING WITH TOLERANCE IN OUR WORLD

It's time, It's time to change both individually and collectively, how you perceive each other... how you treat each other. It is time to drop your differences... What do they contribute to you? That is a question we would like you to ask yourself each time you have a difference of opinion...a different way of seeing something about another human being. If you are able to...if you choose to, come to an understanding of what that difference will mean to you...tomorrow...next week...next month... next year?

You may find that having that difference between you made significantly will separate you, will not bring you together. Is this what you are really choosing for your life, for your time on this planet?

Next time you observe something differently to another…We would ask you to see it simply as that… 'I see this particular thing from a different viewpoint to this other human being' and that is ok, that is in part how your world functions… each person's perspective can be a contribution. It may simply be that their contribution to you is because of their differing viewpoint, this has allowed you to question yours. It may allow you to soften yours, this does not mean that you have to align with theirs…it means that you have reassessed something in you and made a choice to make a change, even if it is a small change.

This small change can then allow you some ease. This ease then has the opportunity to affect your living… the way you perceive…and in doing this, you have much more tolerance for yourself…and those around you in your world. It's time!

# 8 CONNECTING TO CONSCIOUSNESS AND SPIRITUALITY, CONTROL DIVERSITY WITH YOURSELF AND OTHER HUMANS

Being conscious is a state of being that you are all intending towards. While your intentions are put forward with your best intention, as you know you often miss the mark, in your perception. We are saying to you that with your pure intention, you never miss the mark. You always achieve your intention of consciousness. It is only in those moments of less or no intention that you do not achieve your own perspective of how you understand consciousness.

Consciousness is that moment by moment living of your lives that comes from your intention of doing all that you can to make your world a better place. Here we are talking about your inner world - that world inside you where you make your choices from, where you choose everything that you are a part of in the outer world.

If you were to say 'I didn't choose to be in an earthquake, a tsunami, a cyclone, a hurricane or any natural occurrence on this planet'. We would say to you that your inner choices on that day, at that moment had you in a place where these earth changes are occurring. So, your consciousness of your choice to be in this place, in these moments gave you the consequences that occurred for you.

Being conscious is being totally aware in each moment of both your internal choices and the external circumstances that these internal choices lead you to. It was not originally intended for humans to be conscious in every moment, although it is a potential that they can. The energetic and physical shifts on this planet at this time are directly related to the amount of consciousness on the planet at this time.

You all as humans have far surpassed what was perceived as possible for humans and we as your keepers are just so delighted with this as this allows us much closer contact with you all. For example, Pamela is able to channel this message for you. We love our communication with you all and would like to remind you that it is in those moments of intuition that you have when you just 'know' something that we are in direct communication with you.

Some of you may have noticed that you are having these moments more often and this is one way that your consciousness is growing. With these moments of knowing, we suggest strongly that you follow your intuition and act on your knowledge.

The word 'spiritual' encompasses so many perceptions in your world and those perceptions include consciousness. They also include your religions; your personal perception of what God is and everything in between.

Consciousness is your moment by moment way of being, seeing your world and the choices that you make. Living your life consciously allows you more ease as you are aware of choosing for yourself more at the moment. This all attributes to your way of perceiving and being what can be called spiritual.

Any moment that you spend being conscious gathers together with any moment that others spend being conscious to increase the ease by which humans can live on this planet. Of course, these are only words and it is your pure intention by which you live the life that will help you to make the difference in your own being that you are currently searching for.

## AKASHIC RECORDS ON HOW TO LIVE OR WORK WITH DIFFICULT PEOPLE

Human being difficult is a perception of others around them. People that others describe as difficult persons, or are seen as difficult persons are difficult because the others around them allow the 'difficult person' to have their power or what we would like you to call your empowerment. So, is the difficult person the 'problem' or can you as a person living or working with this person change your perception?

You may think at this point that we are asking you to change your perception of the 'difficult person', we are not. We are asking you to change your perception of yourself. So, could it be that you are saying - 'Aren't they the difficult one?.' Yes, it is quite possible that they have habits and traits that you don't like or agree with.

Therefore, is it for them to change or you to change?

We say to you that even when you are having a discordant interaction with others then it is always up to you to check yourself and see what it is that you can change. With a 'difficult person', what is it that you could see/perceive as different?

If you were to ask yourself this and really take the time and make the effort to understand why you see this particular person as 'difficult' then you are able to look at yourself better, have more understanding of yourself. We suggest that you take a notebook and pen and draw a line down your page lengthways, then at the top of a column write the name of the 'difficult person' and at the top of the other column you write your name.

Now let's look at the 'difficult person' first. Why do you see them as difficult - write down everything or reason why you see them as difficult? Then when you are done, go to your column and write down everything or reason that they might see you as difficult, contrary or non-co-operative.

Now if you are able to address this with honesty, you will be able to see and understand that the 'difficult' part in your relationship with them is not all about them. You will be able to see that there are contributing factors that come from 'your side of the fence' as well. We suspect with some humor here, that the 'difficult person' column is a lot larger and more detailed than your column if it's a concept to be true.

Now that you have gotten this off your chest so to

speak and on to paper - we would ask you to take one thing that you have written down in YOUR column and write it in the middle of another page with a circle around it like a 'mind map'. Then draw a line out from this circle and write down how you react in this situation with the 'difficult person'.

You may write that you are anxious around them, so the word 'anxious' would be in the circle at the end of the line that you have drawn. You may write that you have a tendency to hide things [physical, mental or emotional] from them because you fear, or feel anxious about their reaction to this.

Go through your list and write as much as possible so that you receive a larger understanding of your reactions, the ways that you change yourself to accommodate what you perceive as their 'difficulties' and you might even see that some of what you have written is actually written in fear, as you have allowed fear to come into your relationship.

Now that you have a better understanding of the bigger picture of your relationship with the 'difficult person', we are asking you to choose one aspect of this to change. If the aspect of this that you choose to change is your anxiety around them, then the next time that you feel yourself getting anxious; take a deep breath and another deep breath and notice that as you are concentrating on taking a deep breath, for a fleeting few seconds as you are breathing in, your anxiety seems to dissipate. Become aware that the concentration on breathing in allows the anxiety to dissipate.

As you breathe out say silently to yourself, think the word 'love'. Do this as many times as you can in any situation with the 'difficult person', we suggest that five deep breaths would be beneficial. Then check with yourself about how you now feel about the particular situation and the other person. If you can do this simple exercise each time you are in the company of the 'difficult person' for one month and then observe how you feel about this person.

We are not saying to you that you are required to love this person, although the only way to heal this situation is to see it with love. We are saying to you to feel love as you say love, and you will be able to do this with continued practice of your breathing exercise. What you are actually doing is reminding yourself that you love yourself and so there is no requirement for you to react in a way that does not engender love for yourself because of the words or actions of another - in this case, the person whom you perceive as difficult.

As you increase the ease with which you do this, you then allow yourself to be empowered by the situation rather than seeing the other person as having power over you. You are choosing your own empowerment and as you do this, you are acknowledging yourself, love.

## AKASHIC RECORDS ABOUT HUMAN FAMILY

Human families are such a conundrum; they are so diverse and this is how it is meant to be. There are no human families that are the same as there are no humans that are the same. So, this allows you all to celebrate your differences as individuals and in a group like a human family

The word celebrate is interesting here as there are many fewer humans who celebrate their families than those who do not celebrate their families. Many of you in your human form have not understood that you made the choices to come into your particular family at this particular time so that you could experience many situations and be able to make choices about those particular situations.

In any given human family situation you are involved in, you have the choice of your thoughts about this, your perceptions about this and your actions about this. So next time you are in a family situation that you may either feel comfortable in or feel discomfort in, we would ask you to take yourself through this exercise: First, be aware of your thoughts - be conscious of your thoughts about this situation. As these thoughts you are having are your observation of good/bad, right /wrong, they are your perceptions of your world. So, you go from your thoughts to your perceptions, to your choices and then to your actions.

## THOUGHTS ---> PERCEPTIONS ---> CHOICES ---> ACTIONS

What if next time you are in a family situation, you just allow and observe what is happening?
What if you don't involve yourself?
What if you neither agree nor disagree?
Can you understand that your thoughts, perceptions, choices and actions could be different?

In this difference are you choosing consciousness?
How do you feel?
How does your body feel?
Is this different from the usual path that you would have taken?
Can you do this again and again and again?
Would this change your world?

You may then like to write this down in your notebook each time, to help you observe over time the changes you are making. This exercise if practiced can allow you to see human families - your human family - differently. Not all human families have conflict. Sometimes you may look at your family and wonder why you came into this family as your perceptions are so different. You may have family that doesn't have much communication and this lack of communication can frustrate you and you feel that you would like to shake them up and say 'live'.
So, why are you in that human family?

We suggest that in some instances this could be because you being you can allow them to see other possibilities and potentials. They (your family), may have chosen to live this lifetime simply observing what is possible and not choosing to do anything other than what they are doing now - just living their lives as though that is all they are here to do, not wanting or choosing any form of awareness.

What do you do - try to change them? If this has been your tactic, we ask, "Has this worked?"
Have you felt angry and frustrated at how they are and would love it if they would change?
What if they chose to change but not in a way that

you thought was appropriate?
How would you feel about that?

Could you choose to just allow them to be how they used to be and use your impetuousness for change in yourself? If you choose to look at the amazing possibilities that are for you here and then, with your human family, simply love them. The human family is such a vast topic that we could go on for days about it. To love all aspects, choices and actions that are attributes of family. This is why you are in a human family, to LOVE.

## AKASHIC RECORDS TOWARDS BECOMING OUR AUTHENTIC SELVES

Being your authentic selves for humans has often been quite a challenge. Without being authentic, you will find it difficult to connect with others easily. There are some beings on this planet at this time who are authentic, who are their authentic selves. There are many human beings on this planet now that are becoming aware of and aspiring to be more of their authentic selves. The complexities of living on this planet challenge authenticity. How this has been done has been impacted by the media, by all the sources of information that are available to you all at this time. As you take bits and pieces of this information available to you and apply it to yourselves, your life becomes more complex and you simply wonder who you are, how did you get to where you are now and why. When you make different choices that come from simplicity, you are then able to see and be your authentic self.

So, how can this happen to you? You can first simply take some time off and sit quietly, preferably in nature and allow yourself to just be. Sit for some time, although we suggest that you do not 'count' time as you do this. When you have sat for some time, your outside world allows itself to become less and your inner world becomes more. As this happens you are gradually able to see what really matters in your life and what you can let go of.

Ask yourself this: What can I now let go of that no longer has any value in my life for me?

This may be time spent with certain people, in places [like work places] or watching or reading the current 'news', or anything that you perceive is no longer of value to you in your life. It's up to you to discern these and one by one remove them from your life. As you go through this process, you will start to feel you – start feeling your authenticity – start feeling how you really are from the inside of you. This process allows the complexities of your life to fall away and in that space available, it allows the simplicity of your life to come to the fore and as your life takes a simpler aspect, you feel you more. You feel your fuller self, you feel your authenticity. This authenticity becomes your way of life and you being your authentic self is really a gift from you to you and then a gift to all others whom you interact with. They observe and feel your own authenticity, start choosing this for themselves and this then allows for more peace on this earth.

# **AKASHIC RECORDS TO CONTROL RESONANCE IN HUMANS**

Resonance is a feeling of 'knowing', a feeling that all is well with you and your life. When you are resonating with life, you know that you are loved, that nothing in your world can distract you from this feeling and you know that all is well with you.

When we talk to you of being loved, we are talking to you of us in spirit loving you and when you recognize and simply 'know' that this love is here for you, it is always here for you, then you are resonating with your life. It is such a deep knowing inside you that is so peaceful and so full of love for you, that you know you can allow your human cares and concerns to fall away and that all is well with you, that your cares and concerns will work themselves out.

When you allow yourself into this space inside you, we ask you to stay there as long as you can in your human timing as this connection with us allows you peace with your world. This is a beautiful place, space for a human being to be in. You will love this space so much that you will look for it more and more often and as you connect with this space, you will have the resonance of more love, more joy and more ease in your daily lives.

This allows you as an individual to have more peace. More peace in your world contributes to humanity, which then allows more peace on your earth. It just takes you to connect and to resonate with your life for more peace on earth. This is a potential and a possibility we in spirit can see.

## AKASHIC RECORDS TO KNOW YOUR FREE WILL AND WHAT IT MEANS TO US

Free will or free choice is a term that human beings will hear more often as they come to understand that this is what the whole of their life is about. Each of you is given free will or choice to use from the moment you are born. At first, when you are a small human, you do not understand this concept at all even though you in spirit understand it very well and this is one of the enticements you felt like the spirit to come again to this planet. You chose to come again as you see this as an experiment that allows you such freedom of choice.

When you are actually on this planet and as you grow as a child, you come across the experiences born of your use of your free will. As human, you come to understand the consequences in the human form of using your free will. You as a human do not always like or enjoy these consequences. As a child, you learn that adults around you don't like certain behaviors so they use some form of discipline that you do not like.

This goes on throughout your life and as this process happens, you then come to an understanding of the choices that you make and how they play out in your life. As you gain some wisdom, you adjust your choices with your understanding of your free will and this can then help you to have a life that has more ease than conflict.

When this understanding comes to you, you increase your awareness of the choices available to you and choose more intuitively than you may have done in your past. When you do this, you are still using your free will but you are just using more discernment in your choices. You are choosing ease rather than conflict or challenge.

Our suggestion to you is to look at instances in your life where you used your free will and it did not serve you well and have a look at how you could have chosen to use your free will differently and how you would have chosen more ease.

From now on, bring your awareness of this to the surface as you make your choices. As you do this, you will bring yourself more ease by using your intuition processes more and you will have a life that brings you more joy and peace. Can you make different choices from now on?

# 9 RECORDS OF CONNECTION AND CHANGES

Connecting with people, minds, thoughts, and feelings, without prior connection with your true self, it will fail. You must understand yourself before you can connect with others. What am I feeling more? Your Keepers can make you understand better. It is time for you all to choose to feel yourself from the inside, to go inside to make your choices from now on. If you are to look back on some of the choices that you have made that bought you the greatest pain - both physical and emotional, the most discomfort, the most unease, the most un-ease and you have a really good and truthful look at these choices, you may just acknowledge that you made these choices from your head.

You may have made these choices to please others,

to give others what you thought that they wanted. Could you question yourself as to whether you made any of these choices for yourself? In that moment of choice, where was the being of you choosing for you? How could you have changed this and chosen for you, regardless of others opinions, points of view or reactions? You may have allowed this discomfort, un-ease or pain to come into your life because you were not prepared to stand in your own knowledge of yourself and to choose for you.

To change this, take more quiet time - more time in nature - and with this, it will allow you to have a greater understanding of you and what your choices are in your life. As you do this, you will feel more contentment, more ease and less pain, both physical and emotional. This is your life and now is the time for you to make choices for you. You are the one who matters in your life! As you choose for you, others may not like or agree with your choices. If you choose not to align with their choices for you, you will feel a space opening up in your heart center. As you open up to more of, "YOU FEELING YOU" - the energies are within you. This is love for your personality. Do you dare to love yourself at all? Then try something today!

## GOOD COMMUNICATION

The topic is about change, and we would like to approach this a little differently than we have been doing. You all as human beings have become used to change - it has been a current moving through your lives in recent times, just as electricity moves through wires. Electricity moves through wires and what a brilliant invention this has been for humanity. Electricity has given you all so much - the comfort of your body, ease in your physical lives and the area that electricity has been a huge benefit to you, in the area of communication. As you are aware this communication has changed the way you live your lives. It has changed the way we are able to communicate with you.

As many of you now have and use the internet, you can receive information and communicate this information so quickly now. This can and is bringing about so much change. If you are to observe yourself, you will find that each day you make lot of small changes - you make these changes often without being totally present or having a clear awareness of these changes. These small changes are made many times because of communication. You have so much more communication than you did in your past, as you know the internet allows you to communicate instantly with others all over your world. Yes, we hear you saying that this is not new and how can we change more.

What we would like you to observe and consider is that every electronic communication that you make has an effect on your energy, the energy of where you live and how you actually live your life. Now that you as the collective of humanity have established this form of communication which is so perfect for all the changes that you as a collective are pursuing - consider every single communication that you make electronically… Can you change the words and energy that you use so that your message is always one that includes LOVE? And, yes, you may find this easier to do with family and friends whom you enjoy but what about those whom you do not feel so much attunement with? How do you communicate love when you are sending an email at work for example? It is just like smiling when you are on the phone - the energy is communicated. We are not asking you to do or be any energy that is not really you.

We are asking you to ask yourself to write your communication with the energy of love. If you are to make this choice - to send any communications with the energy of love - then you may be surprised at the choices of words that you use, the allowance that you have for others, what you have changed and how you feel about this change. If you choose to make a change - make a difference in your communications with others - you may be surprised with yourself at how you feel about others.

For each of you it will be different — maybe a few cheery words to end your communication or humor in how you address your communication. If you are making a personal communication, and you choose to talk about a situation in your life that you are not comfortable with, at this moment, you have a choice: Are you using blame? Are you choosing to only see one side of the situation? Are you able to ask others how they would see this situation if they were able to observe this with the energy of love? If you are able to ask this, you may gain much help from the wisdom of others. In asking them to access their wisdom to help you, you are also helping them to observe themselves, their real self. There is an opportunity there for both of you, when you choose to allow your communication in the energy of love. Change is available to you all in many areas of your lives and if you communicate in the energy of love, it has the potential to gift to humanity massive change. Are you making a choice for this now? This change of communication starts with you.

## HOW TO TRUST MORE FOR PERFECT CONNECTION

Trust is when each of you learn and understand that trusting yourselves is a key to self-love. To trust yourself, you are required to understand that you are perfect just the way you are. As that center of you, that heart space of you knows itself, feels the true essence of itself and you feel the peace inside, you will then have that absolute 'knowing' inside yourself that all is perfectly OK in your universe, that all is well, and there is nothing to fear. Fear occurs when you do not trust yourself, when you allow what is happening outside of you to affect you. This fear can then be made in the bigger and bigger concepts that are not actually real. As you allow your mind to take this path, your fear increases and your trust decreases. When you are in a situation of simply 'knowing' that all is well with you, even if this is only for a few moments of your time, then you are experiencing trust. Observe these moments because, as you allow these moments to increase, to happen more often, then you are allowing more trust into your life and this can lead to more joy and peace. As you feel trust for yourself, others give you more opportunities to try out trusting yourself more. Others can help you to make the space for your experiments with self-trust so that you easily increase the moments spent in this space and of course those are fewer moments spent in fear. Trust is part of humanity's process as humanity moves into enlightenment. Enlightenment is you seeing the light in you.

## OVERCOMING ANXIETY, THE PULLBACK OF CONNECTION

Anxiety is fear brought on by your perception of your current circumstances. Addressing anxiety will help you overcome your fears and as you overcome your fears, you open yourself up to allow more love in your life. Anxiety is often felt in a part of your physical body. It is helpful for you, if you use your awareness to bring your mind where you feel anxiety first. Many feel anxiety in their stomach, they would say 'I have butterflies in my stomach'. Others feel anxiety in their head, they experience 'panic' and this panic brings their anxiety to the surface. So for each human that experiences anxiety, your first step is to recognize how the symptoms appear for you, in what order they appear. As you become aware of this, you can then take steps to address your anxiety. The next time you notice that your particular symptoms are appearing — STOP, then acknowledge to yourself that you are in the beginning stages of your anxiety and then follow your thought process back to the source thought that started the anxious symptoms so you can have awareness of the process that you take yourself through. The key with this is to catch your thought processes as soon as you can and for you to have a clear understanding of what thoughts you have that produce the symptoms that you call anxiety. There may be a few different physical symptoms in your body. There also may be a few thinking patterns that you have that produce anxiety in you. So, it is important for you to know all of them. Once you have come to an understanding in yourself about your particular anxiety process, it is then up to you to make a choice to change this. How do you make these changes? You take the concept or idea that you have that produces anxiety in you, for example — 'if you are concerned about not having enough money'. We would suggest that you write your concerns, then take each concern separately and have a wonderful look at it — turn it upside down and inside out and then look at your worst fear about not having enough money. When you have taken your thought process to the worst part of your fear, examining your worst fear — ask yourself what could happen and how would you address it or how would you find a solution for this? You may be surprised at your creativity in how you can change your finances around to be able to cope with your worst fear. Because you have done this exercise, you will then understand that you can lessen the fear you have about this particular part of your life.

You may even do this exercise a few times because as you practice it, you will be able to deal with your fears/anxiety more easily each time. Fear or anxiety often appears when there is a change in your life, or you have an expectation that change may happen and you either don't cope with change easily or change sends you into a spin. Any change that comes to you that you are fearful about — do the same exercise — write it down — pull it apart into smaller pieces and then have a look at each part as to how you can cope with it. Anxiety and fear is the same emotion, and they are often in your life because you don't have full information on a particular issue or situation or you do not understand the situation or issue as much as you could. We say to you — ask questions — because when you have more information, you will feel your fear dissipate as your understanding of the situation or issue increases. Your ideal way of dealing with fear is to take the course of action that leads you towards love. You have a choice in the situation — the answer that allows more love into your world is the best solution for a human being. This sometimes may not be the easiest decision to make, just know that as you make this decision, you are able to let go of your fears and anxiety. The more you do this exercise, the easier it gets for you to overcome your fears and anxiety. As you allow more love in your life, especially for yourself, your self-love will dissipate the anxiety.

## KNOWING TRUE PERFECT PEACE THROUGH AKASHIC RECORD

Peace is an energy that many will be interested in, will talk about and will feel more than the energies on this planet continue to shift and change. Peace on earth has been an ideological concept for much of human existence. That is all it has been for most humans, a concept, because humans have not really understood the essence of peace, the feeling of peace or what the real meaning of peace is. This is simply how it was on this planet. Humans liked the idea of peace and until now most humans have had no concept of how peace actually works in individual lives. This is why it has not been possible up until now for you to have 'peace on earth'. For this it is required that peace is understood by every individual before you as humanity can have peace for your world. How can each of you as an individual human beings feel and understand peace? The whole concept of peace is often seen by individuals as something out there, as something that is separate to them as a human being, it is also seen as something that others can or should do. Peace is often not seen by an individual human being as a start with themselves in their lives, in small increments. Up until now the concept of peace has felt too big for each of you to take as being a part of your life that you can take ownership of, responsibility for, and that you can simply 'be peace' in your own environment. To be peace, each human can look closely at their own environment, which includes: relationships, families and friends and your work. How is your peace in your own environment? Understanding peace is all about understanding yourself: who you really are, and what you feel from the inside out about you. When you are able to feel peaceful about you, who you are energetically, physically, emotionally and spiritually, you can then contribute to peace in your world, your own environment and then your contribution adds to peace on earth. As more and more of you can do this then peace on earth is a possibility and a potential for your planet. Feeling peaceful inside of you comes from you making choices about your internal parameters — what is meaningful for you, what works for you. Then choosing to move away from what no longer serves you. As you choose to live your life in this manner, you will find that your internal self will feel more peaceful, your close environment and relationships will feel more peaceful, and you will be contributing to your part of a peaceful world. There is no discernment here between men and women, as both genders have the opportunity to bring peace to this earth. This can be felt by everyone no matter where you dwell on this planet, whether you live in a serene environment or an environment that is more challenging because it is only you who can decide how you feel in your heart. It is time now for each of you to make a decision how you can make changes in your life so that you are contributing to your personal peace, peace with others, and your inner peace. The collective feeling of peace felt on this planet in any moment of your time, makes a contribution to the whole.

## AKASHIC RECORDS FOR UNITY

Unity is required at this time on planet earth. Unity can be gained by each one of you choosing to be with others rather than against others. This may sound obvious and what we find interesting sometimes is that what humans can see as obvious, they often choose not to address. Individuals find it perfectly OK for others to address the issues around unity and then they continue to have situations in their own lives where unity could be addressed and achieved and they choose not to do so. Unity is harmony, unity is love, and unity is peace. How can humans have harmony with each other when they have contrasting opinions about issues and situations in their lives?

Harmony is possible no matter what the situation. How so you might ask? We would say to you that the possibility and potentials for harmony come through choice. As each individual human makes different choices in a situation, then harmony can be present and available for all. Harmony is your personal responsibility, if you are asking for unity which will allow peace in your world. In any situation, if you simply allow the other person their point of view and you understand and allow you to have your own thoughts in the situation in a peaceful way, you can agree to not agree and this can allow harmony in the situation, which can lead to unity. It is when one of you is choosing to be 'right' about the issue or situation that disunity appears. Often when this happens the subject that you were disagreeing with becomes lost in the need of one or both of the opposing sides to be 'right'.

So, the disharmony becomes about being 'right' or 'wrong' and there is no unity in this. Next time you are in a situation where you disagree with another's perceptions, you can choose to: check your own perceptions on this point. Use your allowance to give the others some space to express themselves. Make a choice as to whether you really would like to take yourself to a place of disharmony, allow yourself to accept that others can differ from you and that you have within you a degree of unity that allows your acceptance. This is growth for you. You may find that you can simply acknowledge that the other person has voiced their view and you do not even feel that you are required to say anything about how you feel on the particular topic or situation.

As you allow this in yourself, you give others the

space to see this in themselves and each time you do this you are adding to the unity in your world. This engenders a more peaceful world for you personally as well as adding in that moment to the unity that is world peace. Unity is all about the choices that you make. It starts with you and continues with you throughout your life. Unity is a moment by moment choice. The question will help you to make the choice for unity next time an opportunity is provided in your life.

## HOW CAN HUMANS SHOW GRATITUDE IN THEIR DAILY LIVES FOR LONG-TERM CONNECTION

Gratitude can be shown by humans as they live their daily lives by simply 'being'. Being themselves…being in the moment and allowing others in their lives to just 'be'. When you as humans allow yourselves to 'be', then you can actually feel inside yourselves just how grateful you are for your life, your choices, your family, your friends and all aspects of your living. As you allow yourself to 'be', you allow a stillness to surround you and as you allow this to happen, you then are acknowledging your spiritual being - the part of you that just 'knows' that all is well, that all is being experienced perfectly regardless of the outside appearances of your life or other people's lives.

This 'be'-ing is you knowing your connection with spirit. You as humans often don't feel connected to spirit even though you are in each moment of your day. So, as you experience this 'beingness', you are actually more aware of your spiritual connection and with this awareness comes the understanding, the feeling that all is as it is meant to be. Feeling gratitude takes you to your heart center and this is the place that you feel spirit, you feel the softness, the gentleness and the nurturing of us. As you allow yourself to feel this, you 'know' how your connection to us feels. We would suggest to you all that, for everything happening in your lives, you feel gratitude because even as you feel gratitude for the happenings in your life that you consider negative, that you consider unfortunate, that you 'think' that you have not chosen, there is understanding there, there is learning there and there is love for yourself there as you allow your awareness of this.

Your contribution to healing yourselves is allowance. When you allow change, then your cells and emotions can help you - this comes with choice. When you choose to talk to your cells with love and ask for your headache, for instance, to go, that love that you express for yourself allows your cells to make changes so that your headache can dissipate. If you were to feel anger, frustration or apathy because you have a headache, then your cells spontaneously give you more of what you are choosing. If you were to say to your cells: "I love you, I love myself and I feel gratitude that I can ask you to change what is happening in my body right now. Please cells change what is required to be changed so that my head can feel clear now. Thank you for your help." What if you were to speak to your cells with love and gratitude each time you have a condition in your body that you do not enjoy?

Use this with intent next time you have a bodily

condition that you do not want to continue. Take some quiet time for yourself and see how you can feel differently. If you are in an emotional state that you would like to change, we suggest that you STOP what you are doing, take some quiet moments and ask yourself: Why am I choosing this emotional state? What else can I choose? What would give me joy? And then make that choice with gratitude for having the understanding that you can make the choice. This is how you are able to make changes in your life through choosing and then focusing on what you do enjoy and leaving behind all that no longer serves you.

This is how you can contribute to healing yourself. This is how gratitude and healing play together to allow you to have a life that is your choice and therefore more enjoyable to you.

## WHAT HAPPENS WITH OUR BODIES IN RELATION TO THE SHIFTING ENERGIES ON OUR PLANET

Your human bodies are responding to the recalibration of your planet by recalibrating themselves. Some of you have noticed and some have not. Some of you have noticed because your body feels differently than it used to feel and often you have no words to describe this difference... you just know it. What is happening is that as your planet changes, your bodies require different foods and different exercise - sometimes more food but mostly less food. The recalibration is happening in your cells and this is a direct response as parts of your DNA are becoming more activated as you are making different choices and choices that align more with your energetic self.

What happens is that your food requirements often become less as the spiritual parts of your DNA are becoming activated and this activation allows your body to use more of your spiritual energy to live your life. You may find that you really enjoy a particular food and this food may be a food from another culture than your current culture. This is your Akashic remembrance coming into play. If for example you are noticing that you are enjoying Indian food, this may be because you have had many lives in India and your Akash is giving you a message, a hint. You may like to dress your body in a particular manner that brings into play your Akashic remembrance from other lifetimes and cultures.

As your body recalibrates, you may find that you have unexplained discomfort.... know that this is all part of the recalibration. As the energy changes in your cells, your body may require to release and the discomfort is allowing this to happen. Sometimes, for some of you, your body will feel 'different' as you feel vibrations in your body that you have not been aware of in your past. These moments of vibration can last a few moments or even only a few seconds. Just acknowledge this and be gentle with yourself and understand that this is you moving into the new energies and that all is well. It is now time to talk to your cells.... ask if your body requires a certain food.

You may choose not to eat your food because that is what you have always done.... what you eat. How fast you eat it? How you cook it or not cook it? How much you eat? Ask your body.... 'Body, would you like a mango now?' You will feel a 'Yes' or a 'NO' as your body responds to your asking. It may take a little time for you to have this connection with your body. This 'time factor' may happen not because your body is not responding but because you are not clearing your mind enough for you to 'hear' your body's answer. Ask and wait…. it will only take a few seconds. If you do not get an answer, try taking a few deep breaths that you can feel right down into your belly, then ask again. There may be times when what your body would like will come to you in pictures - you may see a bowl of fruit salad or an egg cooked in a particular way. You will come to understand this conversation with your body and then it's up to you to follow your body's requests.

Can you do this? This process is about releasing control. When you can do this, you may notice that you have more ease with your body, that your body may feel lighter, moves with more grace, that the elimination of your waste products changes and that your wellness increases. Would you enjoy these benefits of recalibration? Expect that recalibration of your bodies will be an ongoing process for some years to come. Enjoy the process and acknowledge the change that is being made available to you. Thank your cells daily for their contribution to your spiritual journey. Your cells feel this appreciation.

## WHEN ALL YOU KNOW AND BELIEVE CHANGES

Changes are happening all over your world and the universe in every micro-second. We often smile with love when we see the resistance that humans have about change in their lives, in their circumstances. You are all evolving as each second of your time passes and you are often unaware of the change that is occurring. When a change happens in your life, maybe in a relationship or situation that you do not like, you become confused, unsettled, uncertain and often very fearful.

Fear is a human attribute and capacity that allows each of you as individuals in differing ways to understand your life differently, to see that you have the ability for JOY, but where does that JOY go to when fear visits you? You allow the fear to consume you and the joy you may have previously felt simply seems to disappear. What actually happens is that JOY is felt in your heart and fear is thought of in your mind. You allow your mind to fill the space of you instead of allowing the space of love to fill your heart and bring you joy. This is what happens when you have a fearful reaction to change. Can you change this fearful reaction? We say to you, Yes, you can.

Do you choose to make this change? Sometimes. If your choice is to be more open to accepting change, we suggest that you make the effort to understand how you are at the moment you start to fear any changes in your life. This fear may appear in your body - in a tensing of a part of your body. It may appear in your mind, in your thoughts as in what you may call a negative thought that is quite small and then you allow it the space in your mind for it to grow into something much bigger than it is. When you come to an understanding of this in yourself, you will then be able to take your fear of change, break it into smaller pieces and allow yourself to address these smaller pieces, one by one.

As you address these smaller pieces in your life, you will find that fear is no longer the first choice when a situation or a relationship in your life changes into something you do not like. By addressing your fear each time, you have a change happening. You will allow more acceptance for change to come into your life and this will give you more ease. As you have more ease in your life about your relationships and situations, you will find that your life still changes and that you can change more easily and flexibly with it and the fear you previously felt will dissipate.

This is all about choices, your choices, so that when all that you know change, you can bring in acceptance and choice, rather than fear and drama. You will be going from your head to your heart. As you do this, you are opening up your heart for more JOY and EASE. We ask you: What is your choice when all you know changes: fear and drama or joy and ease? Make your choice today!

# 10 RECORD CONNECTED TO LOVE AND PEACE OF MIND

## SIMPLICITY OF LOVE

The essence of love has had confusion around it in how humanity and how individual humans understand love and express love. The word love is often used in situations where there is almost no love and this often brings confusion. There is the perception that in a human family, the essence of love is what glues them together as a family. If you come from a family where there was an abundance of love, you can easily understand this concept. The confusion often comes when you come from a family that has not understood the essence of love and this has created all sorts of issues, problems and situations. This confusion was often included before this lifetime contract between a parent and a child, with the solution or the most peaceful way out of the situation being for one or both of these humans to find their way through the relationship with love.

When one of the individuals has been able to see the situation or relationship with love, this can allow the other individual to see the situation or relationship with more peace. This may not resolve the issues completely to the satisfaction of all. It may simply allow more ease and with this ease, acceptance of how things are, what can change and what is not likely to change. The key here is acceptance. If you are to look at your life and have more understanding of the essence of love, you may see that when you gained acceptance of a situation or a relationship, then you understood the essence of love more.

The actual feeling of love can encompass many attributes and capacities which can include: Understanding that you love another human being regardless of their behaviors. That the behavior is simply when the other human being has forgotten to love themselves. Allowance of yourself and others when you do not agree, do not see life through the same eyes. This allowance is love - the love is in the allowing. Acceptance of yourself, as you are able to accept yourself, regardless of others opinions of you, you then have the capacity to be able to have a larger acceptance of others. Acceptance is love. If you are able to bring more acceptance, allowance and understanding into your own life, then you are able to show by example to others what love is to you, how you perceive love and how you have love in your life.

This example then allows them to have some

awareness, which then can bring more ease into their lives. The essence of love is the way in which you choose to live your life. It is the gifts that you give to yourself of acceptance, allowance and understanding. These gifts allow you expression and expansion to encompass many areas of your life and as you are accepting, allowing and understanding, you are sharing the essence of love that you are with all of humanity. This is the simplicity of love.

## MORE UNDERSTANDING ON WHAT BRINGS JOY

"JOY" is a feeling that humans are now beginning to explore more. In your past, joy was a word that was often attached to 'feeling good' although not many of you understood just how 'good' that feeling of joy can be. To most humans, the feeling of joy seems unreachable - just a few fleeting moments felt in your lifetime. It is now possible for you all to feel joy for more moments in each day as you are coming to understand more just what that feeling is and how you as an individual experience JOY personally. So how do you experience JOY personally? Is it waking up happy, hearing the sounds of nature and appreciating the weather no matter what the physical weather conditions are at the time?

Or do you find joy in the company of the people you live with, the delight of the small people in your life? Or maybe there are moments when you just feel that it is wonderful to be alive? There are two concepts of JOY we would like to explore here: one is the concept that joy can be found on the outside of you and the other is the concept that joy is felt and expressed inside you and you can then allow your joy to bubble out and give others the opportunity to explore their own joy. Whenever you see, feel and understand the joy that you feel, that is created by 'outside of you' conditions, you are expanding your joy and you can express your joy. If you were to watch tomorrow mornings sunrise and feel the wonder of your planet, you would feel the joy of this internally and if you choose you can express this externally by smiling, laughing and sharing the moment with others.

There are many ways to express this joy, even that human term 'jumping for joy' could be a way of expressing your delight at the sunrise. When you feel joy internally, you may just stay with the feeling, you may not choose to express the feeling externally. This internal joy could come from you feeling your connection with us in spirit. You may have a quiet moment where you simply 'know' that you are so-o-o-o connected to us and, in your feeling this connection, you allow yourself to have expansion which then brings to you that feeling of joy. Often for humans these moments are hard to put into words. We suggest to you that when you have these moments, it is perfect for you to keep your linear mind out of this and simply just feel and enjoy that expression of yourself.

As you feel these moments more and more - and the possibilities of this happening in these new energies will support you feeling this - acknowledge to yourself that you have felt JOY. Slowdown in your life if you would like to experience joy. Allow yourself the space to experience joy and as you make the choices to do this, you will find that you notice more JOY MOMENTS in your life every day. This will mean that you 'do' less and as you 'do 'less, you may question yourself as to why you think you need to or have chosen to do particular things in your life.

Everything that you choose to do in your day as to whether this particular 'doing' actually serves you or whether you could 'drop' this particular 'doing' so that your life has the space for you to feel JOY. It is all about choices - your choices for you. When you choose to make more choices for yourself, you will become more aware of your moments of JOY. Is JOY a choice for you?

## WHAT IS BENEVOLENCE

Benevolence is the feeling of God inside. When you are in a state of benevolence, you are in a place of love and in this love, you are in connection with God inside of you. The energy of God is love and benevolence. Being in benevolence allows you to have allowance for yourself and to allow others. No matter what is happening in your life, in your current situation, you are able to have an allowance for yourself, not being in judgement of yourself.

When you are not in judgement of yourself, you allow the space for you to be able to not be in judgement of others, so you are allowing love with yourself and with others. You are allowing benevolence. You know that all is well, no matter what the outside circumstances appear to be and you can allow the outside of your circumstances to follow whatever it is that those circumstances require. Within yourself you can allow benevolence, know that you are connected to God and this is how it is.

There will be more opportunities for you all to allow more benevolence into your lives. This is happening with the changing energies and the opening up within each one of you is allowing benevolence to occur. Be benevolent with yourself. Love yourself no matter what and know that you have intent to have an awareness of benevolent situations. With this, acknowledge them within yourself. You have this capacity available to you now - it is your chance to use it. It is your choice to allow in circumstances or situations that in the past you would not have allowed.

This is how you can become more aware of your benevolence. As each of you become more benevolent, your world will have more peace. Therefore, each moment you are in the energy of benevolence, you will have more peace.

## INNER PEACE, HOW CAN IT BE ACHIEVED

Inner peace is a state of being that is not often achieved by human beings, although the potential for this to happen is on the increase. Peace in a human heart is that sense that all is well with you. Even though there may be challenges in your personal world as well as on your planet, you have a place inside of yourself that you can go to that is so still, where you feel you are so connected with spirit, that whatever may be happening in the physical world, it is of no consequence to you. This isn't that you don't care about things in the physical world. It is that you know they all have their place and you, in your own stillness in connection with spirit, can see how they are placed in the whole scheme of the bigger picture. As you are able to hold this stillness and you can hold the space of peace for yourself, it is possible for you to have inner peace.

In this world at this time, there are not many yet able to hold this space. If you have been able to have one moment of inner peace today, then you have made a contribution to peace in your world. Inner peace is gained by you making choices and these choices include making decisions about what really matters to you and letting go of what is not your concern. It is about you choosing the life you would love to live and living this. As you make this choice, you will find that you feel more joy in more areas of your life and this joy allows you ease and allows you more peace. You can feel this by being in nature more - in your garden, your park, a beach or a mountain, whatever part of nature that you enjoy.

Feel how you feel when you soak up nature. This is part of you feeling peace. Peace is best felt by humans, by you allowing one moment of peace to build into two moments of peace and by you allowing these moments space in your daily lives. Rather than seeing inner peace as a thing that you cannot understand or feel, see inner peace as acknowledging the moments of peace that you already have in your life and adding to them. Your communities and your cultures are made up of individual humans who have the ability to make individual choices.

As each of those individuals make a choice for

peace in each and every moment every day, then the potential for peace can be seen on your planet. This potential is already happening and, although it may take a few generations for there to be peace in your world, the humans on this planet at this time are contributing towards this. Although your media likes to tell you what is not happening for peace, we in spirit can see what is happening for peace. We can see that the potentials are increasing and of course each of you has the choice for peace in each decision that you make. You can make a decision that you may particularly like a group, for example a sports team, and, even though you favor this team, this does not mean that you have to be against the other team in the game.

You can just make a decision to support and favor your chosen team - this is just a choice to support one group while you are not thinking, saying or doing anything against the other team or group of people. This can allow peace in your choices. As humans, you always will have choices to make, so next time you have a choice – choose and support without discouraging others. The place to make these choices from is that place of inner peace. When you know yourself, you then understand what allows you a sense of ease in your life and what does not. If you were to choose what allows you ease, then you would also be choosing for what gives you more peace. Peace in your community will come as each of you choose individual ownership of creating peaceful choices for yourself.

## THE ENERGY OF PRESENCE

Some may see presence as the awareness of living in each moment and this is part of presence. Presence for you is also about how each of you is able to simply hold yourself in yourself – in the you that is really you – in each moment of that awareness. How do you do this? Well, staying in the present moment is a challenge for human beings because on your planet and in the lives you lead, you are able to find so many distractions that take you away from you. Knowing yourself allows you more presence in each moment as you live with that moment by moment awareness of your own presence, of who you really are. Who you really are is who you are in those quiet moments that you allow yourself.

The reason why there is not currently a lot of presence in humanity is that each individual human chooses not to take enough quiet moments to really get to know and understand themselves. As you allow you to question you, to just simply be you in your quiet moments, away from other human beings, then you can feel who you really are – you can feel that Spiritual essence of you and this allowing of yourself to acknowledge the magnificence of you and the beauty of your spiritual essence allows you to have presence. Others notice this and make choices to have some of this for themselves even though at times they don't even know that it is their 'presence' that they are seeking.

Often presence is looked for on the outside of human beings – it is looked for in the position held in the community or family, in the material possessions and in seeing your life through another's eyes, rather than allowing all of your presence to come from your spiritual essence. As you allow your presence to come from inside of you, your 'visibility' with others increases. Others see you as having something different in your way of being that they would choose for themselves, if only they understood what it is.

Your presence is something that is felt by others – you cannot have a strong and visible presence if you do not know who you really are. As you grow into who you really are and can stand in this no matter what the circumstances of your life, then you are the presence of yourself. This will improve your love, even with others.

## MY BEING

It is time now for all of you to have more understanding about BEING. You all are used to 'doing', that your concept of BEING and not doing is not developed enough for you to receive the full benefit that you can have for yourself when you make a choice to BE. Being is about being present in your life, about you being in awareness of your life and how it is in each moment. Being brings you to your present moment. When you are in your present moment, then you are able to fully live your life. You will gain more from your life if you allow yourself more BEING. How to BE… that's the question!

Being is often available to you by slowing down and sometimes, depending on your circumstances, coming to a STOP. Although this is not always how it is. Being is about your presence - it's about you having a moment by moment awareness of your life and living. Think back over the last hour of your life and observe just how much doing you did and how much being you allowed. You may have observed that often the doing took up more space in your life than the being. From this moment on - give yourself the gift of BEING. Bring this word and the understanding of the energy that it has into your day. If in your next hour, you allow yourself to BE more - you may find that you feel differently and that all the 'doing' that you require for yourself was 'done' as well.

A few moments of you gifting yourself the presence of you each hour, will make a difference because, in this gift of BEING, you will come to an understanding that you are not required to 'do' as much as you thought that you had to, to do what is required. Your BEING will allow you to engage your simplicity. It will allow you to take some of the human complexity out of whatever it is that you are engaged in. There is a possibility that, if you practice BEING, if you allow yourself to BE more often, that you will find an EASE coming into your life that allows you to 'see' how to simplify your life and give yourself the gift of BEING.

When you are being, your intuition is available to you with more ease - your JOY is available to you and with these two energies you are able to make different choices that allow you more simplicity and ease. Then you can make an allowance for you for more time for you to just BE. A way for humans to increase their BEING is to spend more time in nature... to just sit and observe... to just absorb how nature has really got it together to just be able to be. This time in nature will be so beneficial for you on all levels of your being. You can allow this time to bring you to a deeper appreciation of nature and how nature supports you, of how Gaia supports you. Allow your breath to be slow and to be deeper. Feel the love for those around you.

Acknowledge that God is within you and that you are so-o-o-o connected and supported by us in spirit. When you are able to do this, this allows us to connect with you and help you with what you call your intuition. You may find that, at this time of BEING, you allow your imagination to run. Allow this to happen, as this is your intuition giving you messages that will often save you a lot of doing. You may find your solution much quicker this way. You can connect with the people that will benefit you as you will understand how the connection between the two of you can be an advantage to you both.

Your quiet BEING allows you to appreciate those close to you and this can help your relationships to have more EASE. Mostly you will find that you have enhanced and engendered your connection you have with yourself and this will be your greatest gift in making a choice to BE. That is all it is …a choice you can make. It's up to me to be who I want to be so that you can be free to love.

## KNOWING YOUR VULNERABILITY

Vulnerability is a feeling that you as humans will become more acquainted with. In your daily lives you often cover up your vulnerability as this often shows your innermost feelings. Up until this timing, humans have not understood the value to themselves of being able to show their vulnerability, which gives the human the potential to access a deeper part of their own divine path. When we say deeper, what we mean is that you will be able to take yourself into higher vibrations that will allow you to feel more of who you really are. Vulnerability is covered up in many ways by humans being human.

This cover up can come in the form of anger, depression, unworthiness, low self-esteem, being pathetic, stubborn or silent when communication could help your situation. There are many more ways to cover up your vulnerability than we have listed here... If you ask yourself, you will know how you 'cover up'. You allowing you to be vulnerable in any situation then allows others to be vulnerable. When you do this, this can often help to resolve an issue between you and others. It allows you to honor yourself and your divinity, which then gives others this opportunity as well.

What is vulnerability? Vulnerability occurs in those moments when you open your innermost self up and allow this to be seen and felt by others. It often happens spontaneously when you are in a situation that you really care about and this situation is one that requires some resolution or even acceptance from you. The feeling of vulnerability will come and at that very second, you have the opportunity to honor yourself and allow the feeling through or to squash the feeling and cover up. What do you have to fear in allowing vulnerability through? We say to you that there is nothing, nothing to fear.

In these moments and it is often only moments of your life, if you allow your vulnerability to be visible to others, you are then able to move to a deeper understanding of your divine nature.... you allow yourself more understanding of you. It may be that, next time you have the opportunity for this and you allow the vulnerability through, you will feel a shift in you - you may describe it in human terms as a 'weight off your shoulders'. Too often humans do not allow their vulnerability through because they are humanly concerned with 'what others will think'. It is now time for you to leave this old paradigm behind.

This old paradigm slows your spiritual awareness and no longer serves you. You may notice that it will become harder and harder for you to squash your vulnerability as the new energies on this planet are not conducive to this. We say to you, relax with your vulnerability, allow it to show and feel the lightness that this allows your being. As you do this, it will become easier and easier for you to do and you are in a closer connection with your divine self.

# CONCLUSION

## Encouragement from the Keepers of the Akashic Records

This is so easy for everyone of you to do. The concept of akashic is a knowing concept. Where you push your might to know the unknown. It only takes a moment of you being present.

You just need to create awareness of what is happening in your life. Whenever you are present in your life, then you are able to be with what is currently happening and with your own "being", your awareness of yourself and others is at the optimum.

This awareness is what you require to encourage yourself and others. It is the only identity that will qualify you to easily access your Akashic records.

We encourage you to encourage yourself, both in moments when you think you deserve more, and also in moments when the going feels tough in your life and some encouragement can go a long way. It is in these moments that you require yourself to take the courage out of encouragement and use it so that you can take the next step.

Take a look back in the time-line of your life and observe those moments when you actually did encourage yourself in a moment when you felt that you really required it.

How did this feel to you? Did this self-encouragement to use your courage help you to get to the next step of whatever the situation was at the time? Humans can often only see and understand this in retrospect.

When you are able to see moments in your life that you have required encouragement, it is then easier for you to see these moments in others' lives when they have a requirement of encouragement and then it is up to you to give all the encouragement you can.

Going through your odd moments alone without clue or solution is painful, but if you can understand the world you're in, you will be able to control some aspects of it without struggle.

You will be able to control things in your reach and things outside your reach that belong to you. You know, you can't give what you don't have. You can't give encouragement if all you've been through in life is surrounded by disappointment and discouragement.

How do you give encouragement? Encouragement can be given in many ways: A quiet smile, a nod of the head, eye contacts, a helping hand, words that uplift and there are many more ways to encourage. The giving of encouragement has so many ways that you as humans can express.

The key is to EXPRESS the energy of encouragement. As you express this energy to others, you are also expressing this energy to yourself. Observe how you feel next time you have encouraged another human being and also be aware of how the energy changes between you - this is your love showing.

While you may not verbally express the love that you are feeling in that moment of encouragement, it is felt by both of you as you both allow the feeling, the energy to express. True encouragement does not allow judgement - it fills up the space so that judgement has no place in that moment.

Can you go forward in your life finding ways to encourage yourself first and then encourage others. This expansion of you both allows for co-operation between you both, among you all.

This serves you well as you are living your lives in the new energies available now. Use your courage to step out and encourage others - this will engender EASE and PEACE for you all.

If you can truly embrace the physical world you can see, it will prepare you to be ready to see the other side of the universe you cannot see but feel. By releasing yourself to learn the unknown, you will be given power and might take full control of every aspect of your life.

This is what your Akashic records will help you to achieve. You will know how to embrace life through past events, present, and the future ones.

Akashic records will help you understand yourself better in order to take full control of a world of myth. A world that cannot be accessed by many.

If you're being truthful to yourself, you will go deep in knowing things in your Akashic records.

Be encouraged, be loved, be focused, be determined, be stabled and be free.

If you can put all these characteristics in place and as your targets, you will get a good result from your Akashic records and your keepers will be greatly helpful. Therefore, go into the unknown and fetch your results.

Made in the USA
Columbia, SC
10 April 2020